I0019883

Introduction to AutoCAD Plant 3D 2017

Tutorial Books

This book may not be duplicated in any way without the express written consent of the publisher, except in the form of brief excerpts or quotations for the purpose of review. The information contained herein is for the personal use of the reader and may not be incorporated in any commercial programs, other books, database or any software without written consent of the publisher. Making copies of this book or any portion for a purpose other than your own is a violation of copyright laws.

Limit of Liability/Disclaimer of Warranty:
The author and publisher make no representations or warranties with respect to the accuracy or completeness of the contents of this work and specifically disclaim all warranties, including without limitation warranties of fitness for a particular purpose. The advice and strategies contained herein may not be suitable for every situation. Neither the publisher nor the author shall be liable for damages arising here from.

Trademarks:
All brand names and product names used in this book are trademarks, registered trademarks, or trade names of their respective holders. The author and publisher do not associate with any product or vendor mentioned in this book.

Copyright © 2016 Tutorial Books

All rights reserved.

Download Resource files from *www.tutorialbook.info*

Table of Contents

Introduction

This book introduces you to AutoCAD Plant 3D 2017, which is used to create Piping and Instrumentation diagrams and design a 3D Plant model quickly. AutoCAD Plant 3D is the product of Autodesk. It was first released to help process and power industry in the year 2007. It also includes AutoCAD P&ID. This software is designed to create Piping and Instrumentation Diagrams, and then design 3D Plant model based on the P&ID. A P&ID (Piping and Instrumentation Diagram) displays the connections between the equipments of a process and the instrumentation controlling the process. A P&ID is created using standard symbols. In AutoCAD Plant 3D, you can create P&IDs using symbols related to various standards such as PIP, ISO, ISA, DIN, and JIS-ISO. You can create 3D Models using predefined and user-defined parts. You can then relate the 3D model to the corresponding P&ID. After creating the 3D models, you can use them to generate Orthographic, elevation, and section views. You can also create Isometric drawings, which can be used to manufacture.

AutoCAD Plant 3D is based on AutoCAD User-interface. However, the intelligent 2D/3D symbols and the connected Database are main features of this application. You can use this database to generate reports, create annotations, and so on. When you change the attributes of various symbols, the annotations are updated automatically.

In AutoCAD Plant 3D, you create everything inside a project in order to make your design consistent. You can create a project on a Standalone workstation or a Network. Creating a project on a Network synchronizes your work with your team members. You can also use the validation tools to check any errors inside the project.

Starting AutoCAD Plant 3D 2017

To start **AutoCAD Plant 3D 2017**, click the **AutoCAD Plant 3D 2017** icon on the Desktop. Alternatively, click the Windows icon at bottom left corner, click the down arrow in the Start screen, swipe or scroll to the **AutoCAD Plant 3D 2017** section, and click the **AutoCAD Plant 3D 2017** icon.

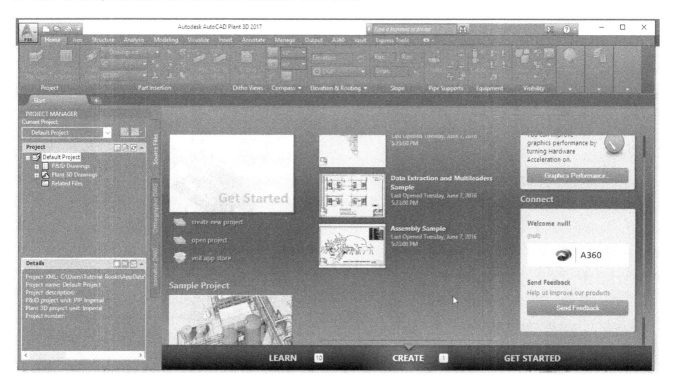

An Overview about Projects in AutoCAD Plant 3D

AutoCAD Plant 3D is a project-based application. It stores each and every object in the Project database. The **Project Manager** palette helps you to access the project files from the database and work inside a project. You can examine the Sample Project to get an overview about the project workflow. Click **Sample Project** on the initial screen to load it in the Project Manager. The Project Manager consists of many drawing types namely, P&IDs, 3D piping, orthographic drawings, and isometric drawings. Also, there are some additional files such as spreadsheets. The program arranges all these data in different tabs on the Project Manager: **Source Files**, **Orthographic DWG**, **Isometric DWG**. On the **Source Files** tab, the P&IDs, 3D Piping, and related files are arranged in a folder hierarchy. The **Orthographic DWG** tab contains the plan view and elevation drawings. The **Isometric DWG** tab contains isometric and spool drawings arranged in folders. The orthographic and isometric drawings are created from the 3D Model.

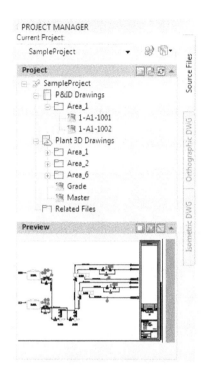

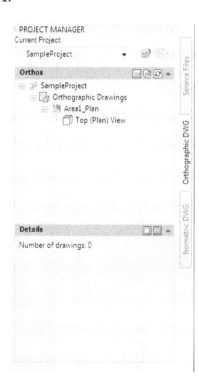

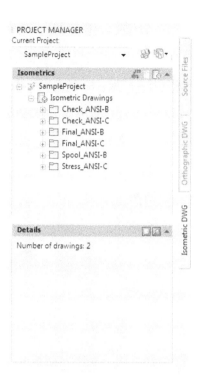

Tutorial 1

In this tutorial, you start a project and then create a P&ID (Piping and Instrumentation Diagram).

Creating a New Project

The first step in the design is to create a project. The project has a set of files and standards.

1. Start AutoCAD Plant 3D 2017.

2. On the initial screen, click **create new project** under the **Get Started** section.

3. Enter **TUTORIAL PROJECT** in the **Enter a name for this project** field.

4. Specify the location of the program generated files and supporting files.

5. Click the **Next** button; the **Specify unit settings** page appears

6. Select **Imperial** to define the units for project drawings.

7. Click the **Next** button; the **Specify P&ID settings** page appears.

8. Specify the directory to save the P&ID files.

9. Select **PIP** as the P&ID symbology standard to be used.

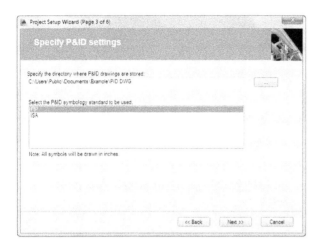

10. Click the **Next** button; the **Specify Plant 3D directory settings** page appears.

11. Click the **Next** button; the **Specify database settings** page appears.

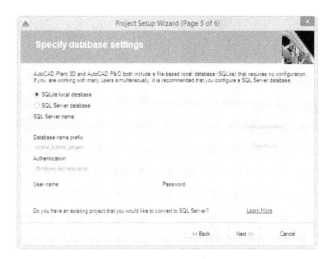

12. Select the **SQLite local database** option if you are working on a standalone workstation.

13. If you are working on a server, select the **SQL Server database** option and configure the server settings.

14. Click the **Next** button; the **Finish** page appears.

15. Click **Finish** to create a new project.

If you want to open an already existing project, then select **Open** from the drop-down on the **Project Manager** (or) On the ribbon, click **Home > Project > Project Manager > Open Project**.

On the **Open** dialog, browse to the location of the project and select the .xml (extendable markup language) file. This file stores all the information of the project. It is recommended that you should not edit or rename this file.

Note that you can open only one project at a time. If you want to open another project, then you need to close all the files related to the currently active project.

In AutoCAD Plant 3D, you need to use the **Project Manager** to open or create a file. You avoid using the **New** and **Open** icons of the AutoCAD application.

Creating a New Drawing

Once the project is created or opened, you can create new drawings using the Project Manager. The Project Manager helps you to create new drawings with all the standards built in it.

1. Right-click on **P&ID Drawings**, and then choose **New Drawing.**

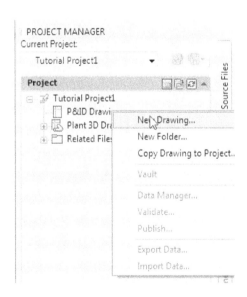

The **New DWG** dialog appears.

2. Enter **Tutorial1** in the **File name** field.

    The **PID ANSI D - Color Dependent Plot Styles.dwt** is the default template. You can select any other template by clicking the **Browse** button next to the **DWG template** field.

3. Click **OK** to create a new P&ID file.

The default screen of the Plant 3D file appears as shown.

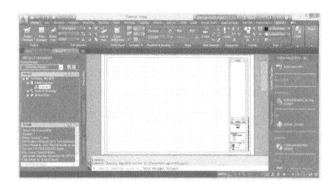

By default, the color scheme of the user interface is **Dark**. You can change it to **Light** if you prefer a bright user interface. To do so, right click and select Options. On the **Options** dialog, click the **Display** tab and select **Color scheme > Light** from the **Window Elements** section. Click **OK** to change the color scheme.

See the lower section of the Project Manager. You can view the details, preview, and work history of the currently opened file.

Also, notice that **Tool Palette** appears at the right side of the screen. You can change the tools displayed on the **Tool Palette**. Right-click on the title bar of the **Tool Palette** to display a shortcut menu.

If you cannot see the P&ID PIP tool palette, click **P&ID PIP** on the shortcut menu.

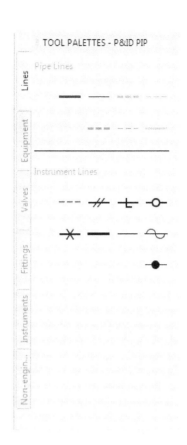

Changing the Workspace

A Workspace is the arrangement of tools and options used for a specific purpose. By default, the Plant 3D Workspace is activated in AutoCAD Plant 3D. You can change the Workspace to PID PIP by clicking the Workspace Switching down arrow at the right-side on the Status bar, and then selecting PID PIP from the flyout.

Viewing the Drawing Properties

1. To view the drawing properties, right-click on the drawing file and select **Properties**; the **Drawing Properties** dialog appears.

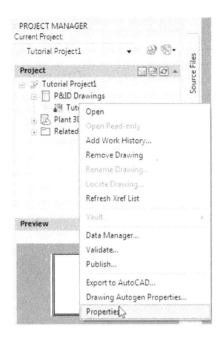

2. Change the properties on the **Drawing Properties** dialog, and then click **OK**.

If you want to open an already existing drawing file, then expand the P&ID Drawings or Plant 3D Drawings folder and double-click on the drawing file. You can also right-click and select **Open**.

If two or more people are working on a project, then only one person can edit the drawing file at a time. If the other person wants to open the file opened in another workstation, then he/she can use the **Open Read-Only** option.

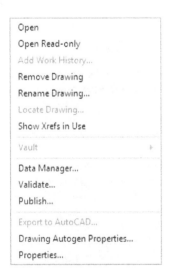

P&ID Symbology Standards

The design process in AutoCAD Plant 3D starts with a P&ID (Piping and Instrumentation Diagram). It helps you to understand the process very quickly. While creating a P&ID, you add data to the drawing. You can also add this data while creating a 3D model. However, in AutoCAD Plant 3D, you add data to a P&ID and later link this data to the 3D model.

In simple AutoCAD, the P&IDs can be created using various symbol blocks. You create these blocks based on the industry standard used in your country/region.

In AutoCAD Plant 3D, there are different symbol libraries available based on five standards. These standards are PIP(Process Industry Practices), ISO(International Standard Organization), ISA(Instrument Society of America), DIN(Deutsches Institut für Normung), and JIS-ISO(Japan Industrial Standard). Each standard has different symbols. For example, the Centrifugal Pump symbol in different standards varies, as shown.

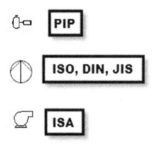

You need to choose a standard while starting a project. You can use only the selected standard throughout the project. So, select a right standard while creating a project.

Placing Equipment

You can start the process of creating a P&ID by first placing the Equipment symbols. After that, you create lines, place inline equipment, place instrumentation, and create annotations.

In this section, you learn to place equipment. AutoCAD Plant 3D provides you with the various pre-defined equipment. The **Equipment** Tool Palette contains all these equipment.

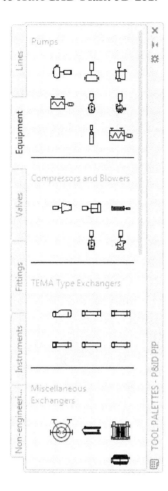

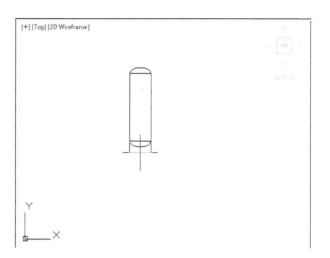

1. On the Tool Palette, select the **Equipment** tab.
2. Click the **Vessel** icon under **Vessels and Miscellaneous Vessel Details.**

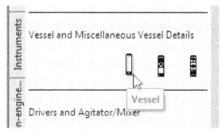

3. Click in the middle of the drawing area to define the vessel location.

Note: You can turn ON or OFF the grid by clicking the Display grid ▦ icon located on the Status bar.

4. Type 1.5 at the scale prompt and press **Enter** key to specify the scale factor.

The **Assign Tag** dialog appears.

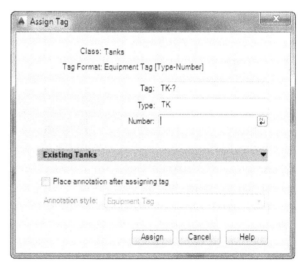

You can type-in information on this dialog, and then assign it to the P&ID component. The program stores the information in the project database. You can then use the Data Manager to view, modify and export this information.

5. On the **Assign Tag** dialog, click the button next to the **Number** field.

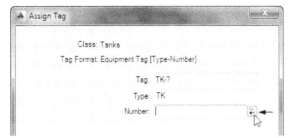

6. Select the **Place annotation after assigning tag** option.
7. Set **Equipment tag** as **Annotation style**.

8. Click **Assign** on the **Assign tag** dialog.
9. Click above the vessel to place the annotation.

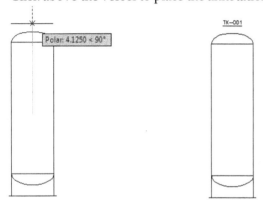

10. Next, place a Horizontal Centrifugal pump
11. To place a pump, click the **Horizontal Centrifugal Pump** icon under the **Pumps** section.

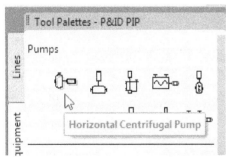

12. Click somewhere near the bottom left of the vessel.

13. Click the button next to the **Number** field.
14. Click **Assign**. The program assigns the tag information to the pump.
15. Place the tag below the pump.

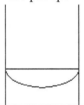

16. Select the pump and its tag by dragging a window.

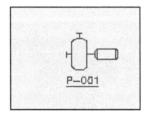

17. Type-in **COPY** in the command line and press Enter.
18. Select the node of the horizontal nozzle of the pump.
19. Move the pointer rightward and click to copy the pump. Press Esc.

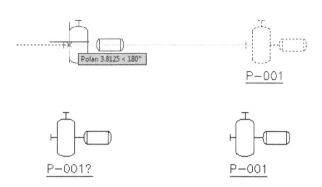

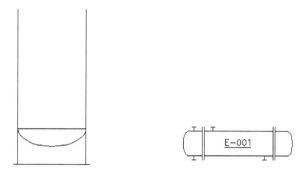

24. The P&ID after placing all the vessels looks, as shown.

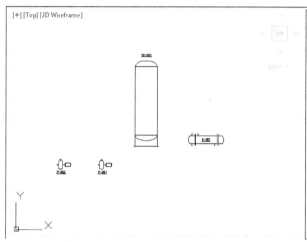

Notice the question mark on the copied tag. To solve this, you have to update the tag.

20. Right-click on the pump and select **Assign Tag**.

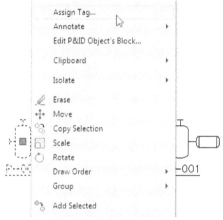

Editing the P&ID Symbols

During the design process, you may require editing the existing P&ID symbols. In this example, you modify the vertical vessel.

1. To edit the vertical vessel, right-click on it and choose **Edit P&ID Object's Block.**

21. Click the button next to the **Number** field and clear the **Place annotation after assigning tag** option.

22. Click **Assign**.

The AutoCAD Block editor appears.

23. Likewise, place a TEMA type BEM Exchanger on the right side of the vessel.

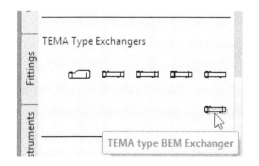

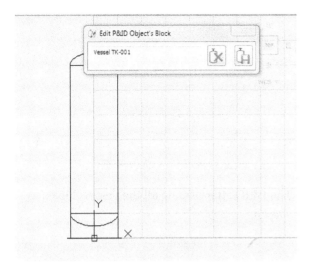

2. Create a selection box and select the dome of the vessel. Press **Delete** to delete the selection.

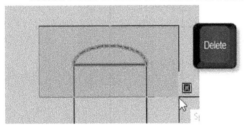

3. Select the left vertical line of the vessel.
4. Click on the top endpoint grip and drag it downwards.
5. Type 2 and press Enter to reduce the length of the line.

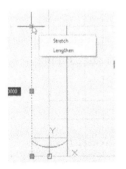 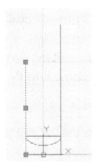

6. Likewise, reduce the length of the right vertical line.
7. Type-in **L** in the command line and press Enter. Create an inclined and vertical line on the left side.
   - Activate the **Polar Tracking** icon on the status bar.
   - Click the down arrow next to the **Polar Tracking** icon and select 30 from the menu.

- Select the top end point of the left vertical line.
- Move the pointer and pause when a traceline appears at 60 degree inclination.
- Move the pointer along the traceline up to a short distance, and then click; an inclined line is created.
- Move the pointer vertically up and click to create a vertical line.

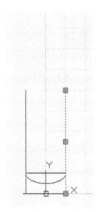 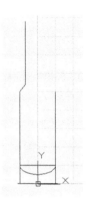

8. Type-in MI in the command line and press Enter. Mirror the newly created lines about the Y-axis.
9. Create a horizontal line connecting the endpoints of the top vertical lines.

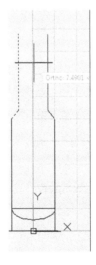 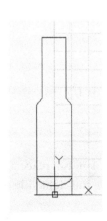

10. Draw other entities, as shown next.

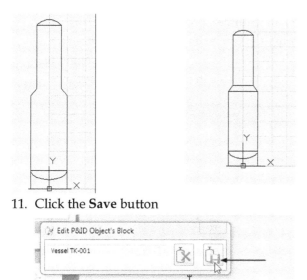

11. Click the **Save** button

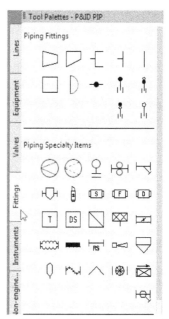

2. Click the **Flanged Nozzle** icon under the **Nozzles** section.

Vessel TK-001

The P&ID symbol after editing is displayed next.

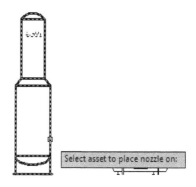

3. Click on the outline of the vertical vessel.

Adding Nozzles to the Equipment

Nozzles are required to connect equipment with a pipe. The program adds Most of the nozzles when you connect equipment with a pipe. Sometimes, you may need to add nozzles to equipment, manually.

4. Define the insertion point, as shown in figure.

1. To add nozzles to equipment, click the **Fittings** tab on the Tool Palette.

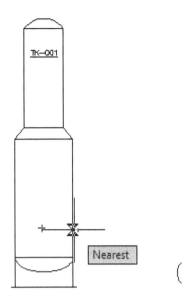

5. Enter 0 as the angle of rotation.

6. Likewise, place another nozzle on the vessel.

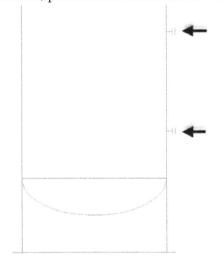

7. To add an annotation to the nozzle, select it, right-click, and then select **Annotation > Tag**.

8. Click **Assign** on the **Assign Tag** dialog, and then place it below the nozzle.

9. Likewise, add the annotation tag to the second nozzle.

Creating Schematic Lines

Schematic lines are the important part of a P&ID. They are used to connect the equipment symbols. The schematic lines, which represent actual pipelines are very different from AutoCAD lines and polylines. They store piping data such as size,

spec, line number, process, and so on. This information can be linked to 3D pipelines. In AutoCAD Plant 3D, you can create pipelines using the tools available in the **Lines** tool palette.

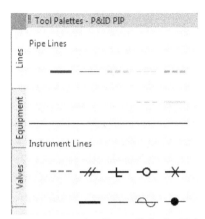

1. To create a pipeline, click the **Primary Line Segment** icon under the **Pipe Lines** section.

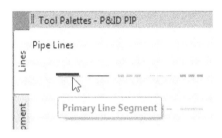

2. On the status bar, click the down-arrow next to the **2D Snap** icon and select the **Quadrant** option.

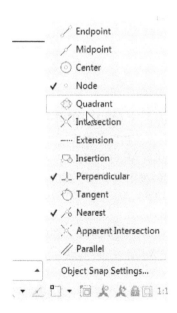

3. Click on the top portion of the vertical vessel.

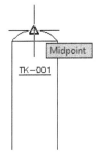

4. Move the pointer upward and click.
5. Move the pointer right-ward and click. An arrow appears at the endpoint of the line, which represents the flow direction of the pipeline.
6. Press **Enter** key.

Notice that the program creates nozzles automatically.

7. Click the **Primary Line Segment** icon and select the nozzle of the pump, as shown in figure.

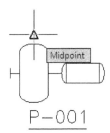

8. Move the pointer upward and click.
9. Move the pointer right-ward and click on the vessel.

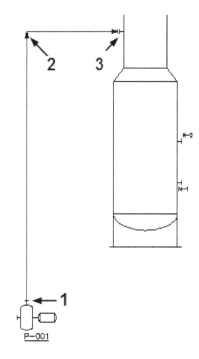

10. Likewise, create a line between the two pumps

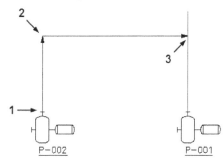

11. Create an inlet pipeline connected to the pump.
   - Click the **Primary Line Segment** icon on the Tool Palette.
   - Specify the first point, as shown.
   - Move the pointer horizontally and specify the second point, as shown.
   - Move the pointer vertically upward.
   - Place the pointer on the inlete nozzle of the pump; a traceline appears.
   - Click on the traceline to create a vertical line.
   - Move the pointer horizontally toward right and select the node of the inlet nozzle.

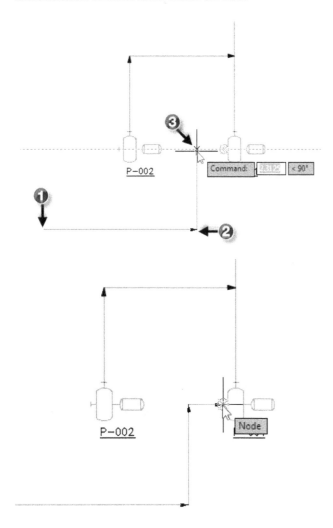

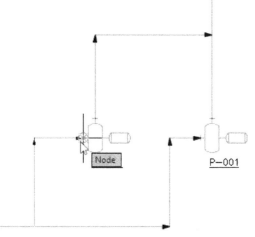

13. Create the other pipelines in the P&ID.

12. Create an inlet pipe connecting the other pump.

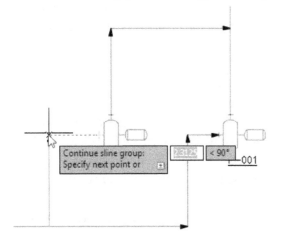

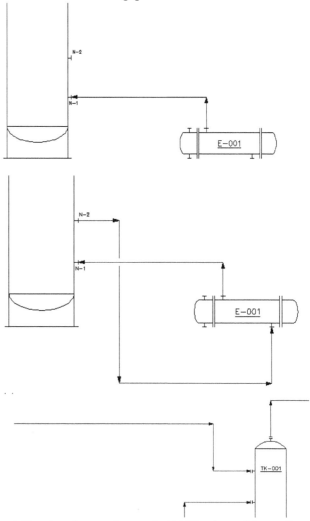

The following figure shows the P&ID after adding all the lines.

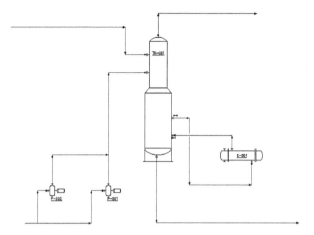

Assigning Tags to lines

In a P&ID, the lines represent the pipes in the real plant. You have to show the information related to the pipelines by assigning tags.

1. Click the **Assign Tag** button on the **P&ID** panel of the **Home** ribbon.

2. Select the inlet line of the pumps.

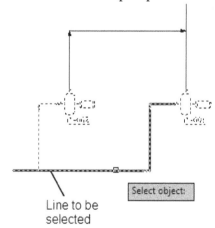

Line to be selected

3. Press Enter key. The **Assign Tag** dialog appears.
4. Enter the following information in this dialog.
   Size: 6"
   Spec: CS300
   Pipe Line Group Service: P
   Pipe Line Group Line Number: 001

5. Select the **Place annotation after assigning tag** option and click **Assign**.

6. Place the annotation below the line.

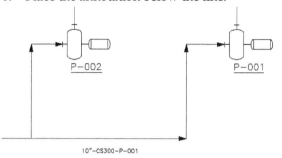

Next, you have to group two lines and assign a tag to them. By grouping lines, you create an association between different line segments. In addition, the grouped line segments have the same line number.

7. To group lines, click the **Make Group** button on the **Line Group** panel of the **Home** ribbon.

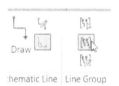

8. Select the lines connecting the vessel and the pumps.

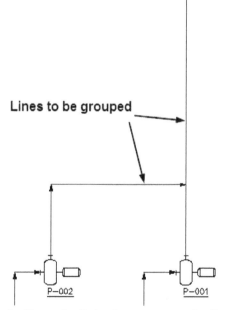

Lines to be grouped

9. Press the **Enter** key to group the lines.

   You can also edit a line group using the **Edit Group** command (on the ribbon, click **Home > Line Group > Edit Group**). Activate this command and select the line group to edit. The command line provides five options (**Add**, **Remove**, **Ungroup**, **Linenumber**, and **Service**).

10. Right-click on the line connected to the pumps and the vertical vessel.

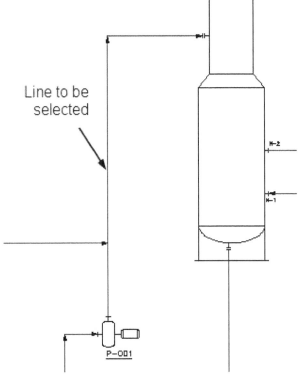

11. Select **Assign Tag** from the shortcut menu to open the **Assign Tag** dialog.
12. Enter the information in the **Assign Tag** dialog, as shown.

    Size: 4"
    Spec: CS300
    Pipe Line Group Service: P
    Pipe Line Group Line Number: 002

13. Place the annotation next to the line.

14. Place the pointer on the pipe connecting the second pump. The information related to the pipe appears.

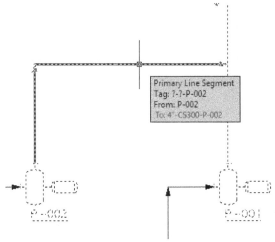

Notice that the tag information is partially applied to the line. You have to specify the line size and spec of the pipeline.

15. Right-click on the line and select **Assign Tag** from the shortcut menu.

16. Enter the **Size** and **Spec** in the **Assign Tag** dialog.

    Size: 4"
    Spec: CS300

17. Click **Assign**.

18. Place the tag above the line.

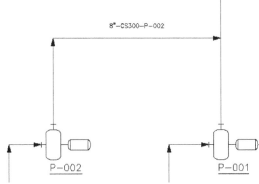

19. Likewise, add tag information to other lines in the P&ID.

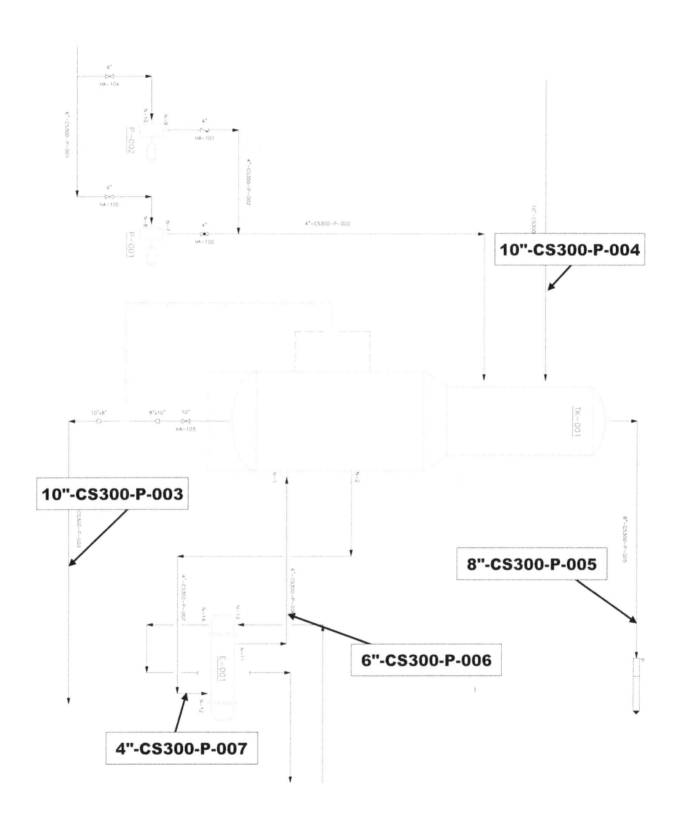

P&ID Painter

In AutoCAD 2017, you can specify the color of a P&ID component based on its size or service for which it is used.

1. On the ribbon, click **Home > P&ID Painter > Paint by Property**.

2. On the **P&ID Painter** panel, select **Color by Service** from the **Painter style** drop-down; the color of the P&ID components changes based on their service.

3. Likewise, select **Color by Size** from the **Painter style** drop-down to change the color based on size.

Placing Valves and Fittings

After creating schematic lines, you can add inline equipment such as valves and fittings. You place inline symbols on a schematic line. When you move the line, the inline symbols move along with it. You can find valve and fitting symbols on the **Valves** tab and **Fittings** tab, respectively.

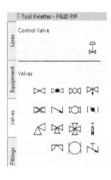

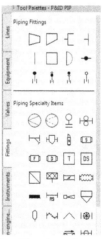

1. To place a check valve, click the **Check Valve** icon on the **Valves** tool palette.

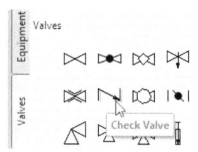

2. Move the pointer on the line and you notice that the valve is aligned with the line.

3. Place the valve on the line connecting the pump. You notice that the valve is attached to the line. In addition, the tag is added to the valve and placed beneath it.

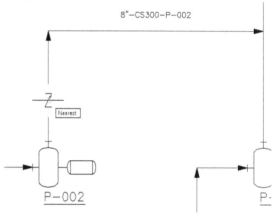

4. Place another check valve.

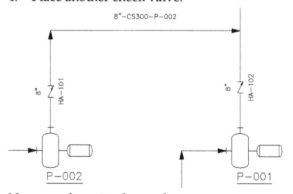

Now, you have to place reducers.

5. To place a reducer, click the **Fittings** tab on Tool Palettes.

6. Click the **Concentric Reducer** icon under the **Pipe Fittings** section.

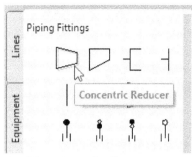

7. Place it on the line connecting the bottom of the vessel.

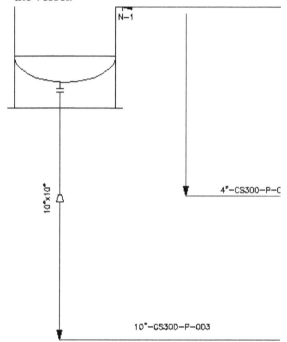

8. Click the **Assign Tag** button on the **P&ID** panel of the **Home** ribbon.

9. Select the line segment below the reducer.

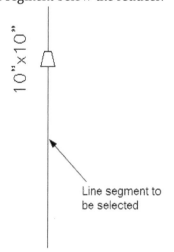

10. Press **Enter** key.
11. In the **Assign Tag** dialog, change the **Size** to 8″.

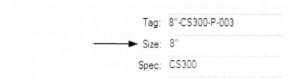

12. Clear the **Place annotation after assigning tag** option.
13. Click **Assign**.

The orientation of the reducer changes.

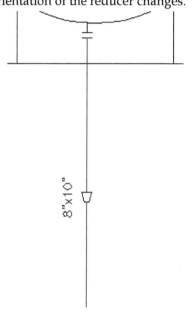

14. Place another concentric reducer at the location shown below

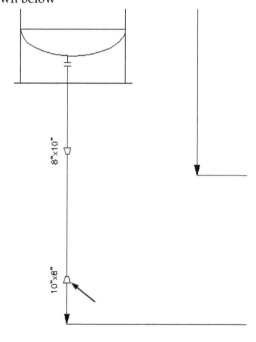

Next, you have to place a gate valve.

15. To place a gate valve, click the **Gate Valve** icon on the **Valves** tool palette.

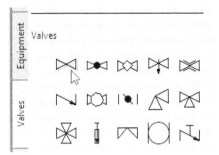

16. Place it at the location shown in figure.

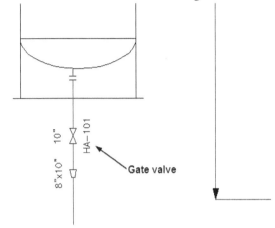

17. Likewise, place valves on lines connecting the pumps.

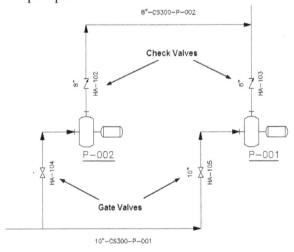

Placing Instruments

In a P&ID, the instrumentation that controls the operation of the plant equipment is represented by the instrument symbols. You can find these symbols on the **Instruments** tool palette. There are many sections on this tool palette, which are based on the use of the instrument symbols.

The **Control Valve** section contains the control valve symbol.

The **Relief Valves** section contains the symbols of various pressure relief valves.

The **Primary Element Symbols (Flow)** section contains the symbols related to flow measuring instruments.

The **General Instruments** section contains the instrument symbols related to the process control instruments.

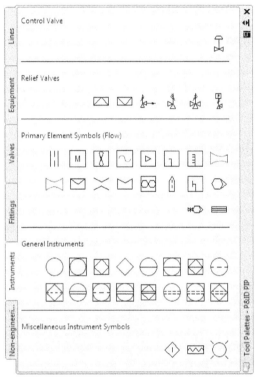

1. To place a control valve, click the **Control Valve** icon on the **Valves** tool palette.

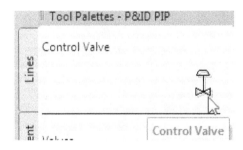

The **Control Valve Browser** appears.

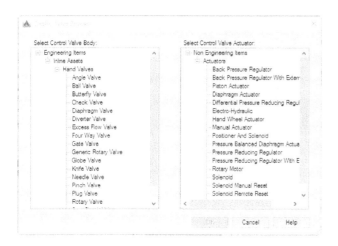

If the **Control Valve Browser** does not appear, select the **Change body or actuator** option from the command line.

2. In the **Control Valve Browser**, select **Gate Valve** as the **Control Valve Body**.

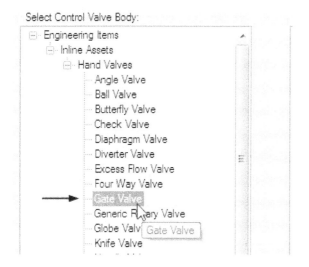

3. On the dialog, click **Non Engineering Items > Actuators > Piston Actuator** under the **Select Control Valve Actuator** section.

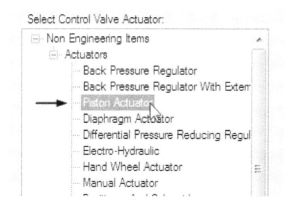

4. Click the **OK** button.
5. Place the control valve at the location shown in figure.

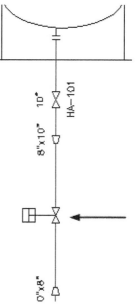

6. Place the annotation balloon
   The **Assign Tag** dialog appears.
7. On the dialog, uncheck **Place annotation after assigning tag**.
8. On the **Assign Tag** dialog, type in the values, as shown.

Follow the steps given next, if the **Area**, **Type**, and **Loop Number** fields are disabled on the **Assign Tag** dialog.

- On the ribbon, click **Home > Project > Project Manager > Project Setup**.

- On the **Project Setup** dialog, click **P&ID DWG Settings > PID Class Definitions > Engineering Items > Instrumentation**.
- On the **Class Settings: Instrumentation** page, under the **Properties** section, uncheck the **Area**, **Type**, **Loop Number** boxes in the **Read Only** column.

- Click **OK**.

9. Click the **Assign** button, and place the tag below the control valve.
10. On the Edit Annotation dialog, specify the values, as shown, and click **OK**.

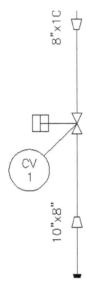

Creating Instrumentation Lines

Instrumentation lines are used to connect the instrument symbols with the P&ID equipment and pipelines. You can create instrumentation lines by picking them from the **Instrument Lines** section on the **Lines** tool palette.

1. To create an electric signal line, click the **Electric Signal** line from the **Instrument Lines** section on the **Lines** tool palette.

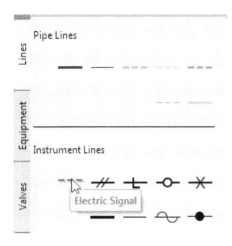

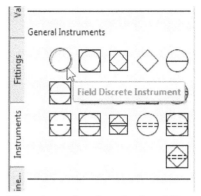

2. Place it on the electric signal line.

2. Select a point on the lower-left portion of the vessel.
3. Move the pointer toward left and select the second point.
4. Move the pointer downward and select the third point.
5. Move the pointer toward right and select a point on the vessel.

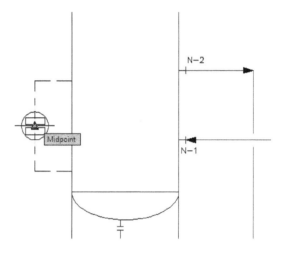

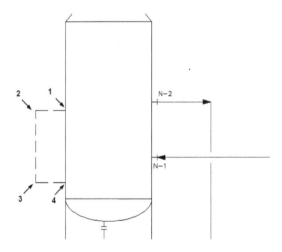

The **Assign Tag** dialog appears.

3. Enter the tag information as shown in figure.

Placing the Field Discrete instrument symbol

1. To place a field discrete instrument symbol, click the **Field Discrete Instrument** icon from the **General Instruments** section on the **Instruments** tool palette.

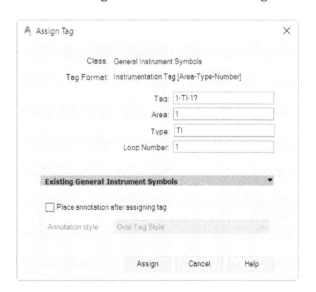

4. Click the **Assign** button.

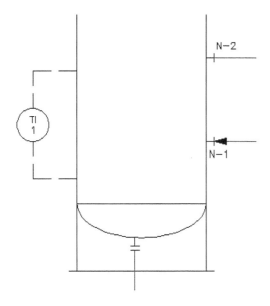

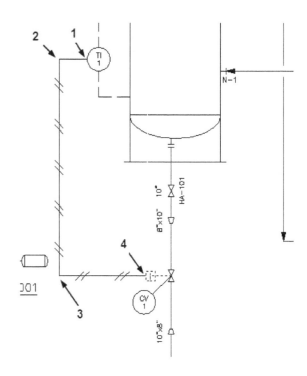

Creating the Pneumatic Signal lines

1. On the **Lines** tool palette, under **Instrument Lines** section, click the **Pneumatic Signal** icon to create pneumatic lines.9248155337

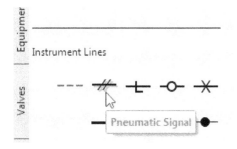

2. Select a point on the **Temperature Indicator** symbol.

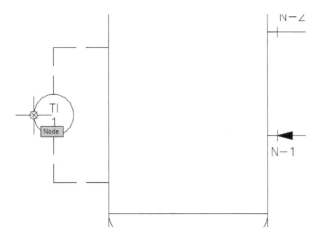

3. Connect the signal line with the control valve.

Adding Off page connectors

In this section, you add off-page connectors. Usually, the P&ID of a project is divided into multiple P&IDs. Therefore, you should maintain a connection between the P&IDs. Off page connectors are used to connect the P&IDs.

1. To add an off page connector, click the **Non-engineering** tab on the Tool palette.

2. Click the **Off Page connector** icon on the **Non-engineering** tool palette.

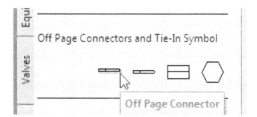

3. Zoom into the off page connector.

4. Select the end point of the line connecting the top portion of the vessel, as shown.

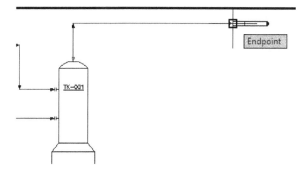

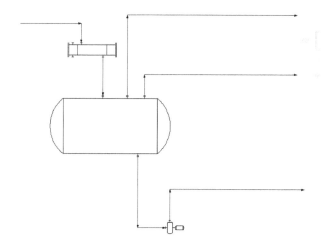

The off page connectors can be used to open the drawing file connected to the currently opened file, quickly. You learn how to connect two off page connectors in the next tutorial.

Checking the Drawing

1. Click the **Drawing Checker** button on the **Validate** panel of the **Home** Ribbon.

The program checks the drawing for any inconsistencies with the project.

2. Click the **Save** button on the **Quick Access Toolbar**.

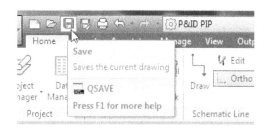

Tutorial 2

In this tutorial, you create a P&ID shown in Figure.

1. To create a new P&ID drawing, select the **P&ID Drawings** node in the **Project Manager** and click the **New Drawing** button.

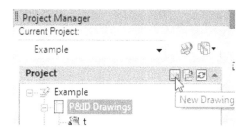

The **New DWG** dialog appears.

2. Enter **Tutorial 2** in the **File name** field and click **OK**.

Creating a Custom symbol and converting it into a P&ID symbol

1. Create the symbol shown in below figure using the **Line** and **Arc** command. Do not apply the dimensions. Dimensions are for your reference only.

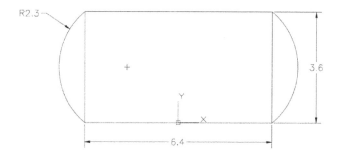

2. Select all the entities of the symbol by dragging a window.

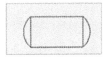 

3. Right-click and select **Convert to P&ID Object**.

The **Convert to P&ID Object** dialog appears.

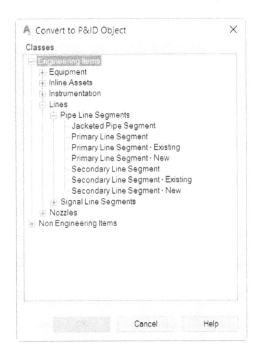

4. Expand the **Equipment** class and select **Tank > Vessel**.

5. Click **OK**.

Next, you have to select the insertion base point.

6. Press and hold SHIFT key and right-click.

7. Select **Midpoint** from the shortcut menu.

8. Select the midpoint of the lower horizontal line.

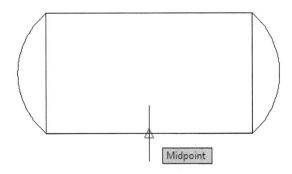

The custom symbol is converted to a P&ID object.

9. Select the symbol and move it to the left side of the drawing sheet.

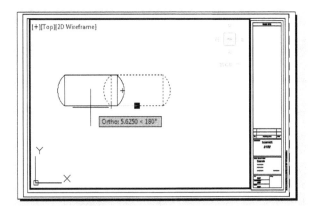

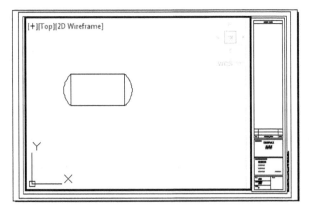

You can also convert regular lines or polylines into P&ID Schematic lines. For example, create lines and arcs using the LINE and ARC command. Next, join them using the JOIN command. You can also use the

POLYLINE command to create the continuous lines and arc.

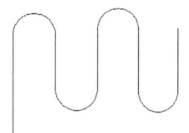

- Select the lines and click the right mouse button.
- Select the **Convert to P&ID Object** option.
- On the dialog, select **Lines > Pipe Line Segments > Primary Line Segment** and click **OK**.

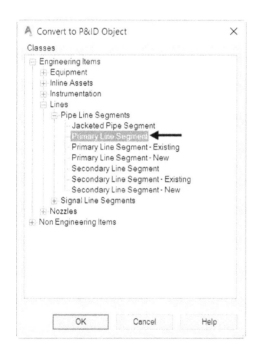

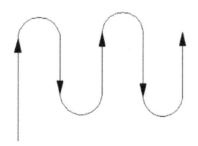

10. Select the **TEMA Type NEN Exchanger** from the **TEMA Type Exchangers** section on the **Equipment** tab.

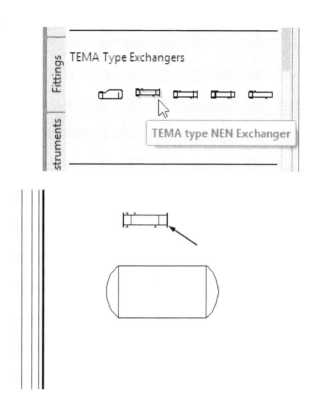

11. Place a Horizontal Centrifugal pump.

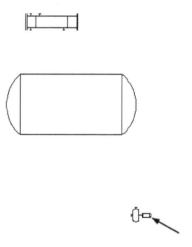

Next, you have to draw the pipelines.

12. Click the **Primary Line Segment** icon under the **Pipe Lines** section of the **Lines** tool palettes.

13. Draw the pipeline connecting the equipment symbols.

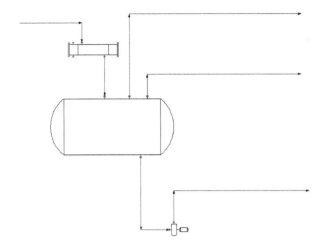

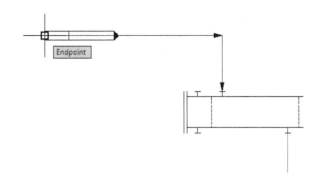

Creating the Secondary Line Segments

1. Click the **Secondary Line Segments** icon on the **Lines** tool palette and create the secondary line segments, as shown next.

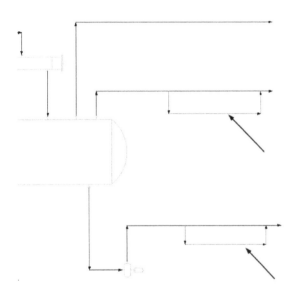

2. Click the **Off Page connector** icon on the **Non-engineering** tool palette.

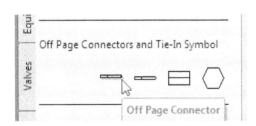

3. Select the end point of the line connecting the heat exchanger, as shown.

Connecting the Off page connectors

1. To connect off page connectors, select the off page connector located at the top left.

2. Click on the (+) plus symbol displayed on the off page connector and select **Connect To**.

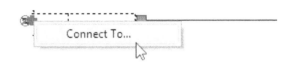

The **Create Connection** window appears.

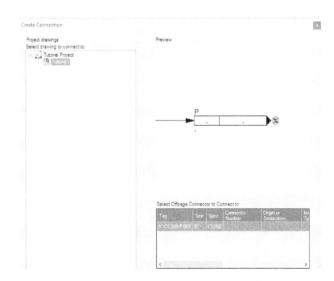

You notice that the off page connector located in the **Tutorial1.dwg** is selected, by default.

3. Press Enter.

The off page connector is connected. However, you notice that an error symbol appears at the end of the off page connector.

4. To solve this error, right-click on the off page connector and select **Off page connector > View connected**.

The **View Connected Off page Connector** dialog appears.

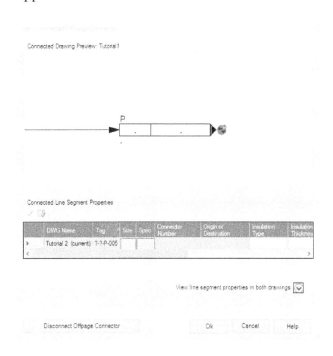

You notice that the **Size** and **Spec** fields are highlighted in this dialog. You need to specify the

size and spec of the line connected to the off page connector of the **Tutorial2.dwg**.

5. Click in the Size field, right-click, and then select **Accept**.

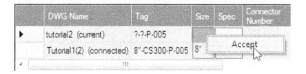

The sizes of the two lines are matched.

6. Likewise, match the spec.

7. Click the **OK** button to solve the error.

8. Click the **Save** button on the **Application Menu**.

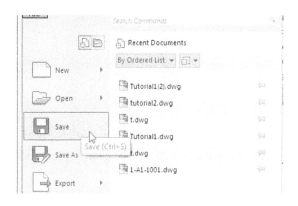

Exercise 1

In this exercise, open the Tutorial2 P&ID and add valves, fittings, instruments and instrumentation lines, and tags. Various regions of the P&ID are given in following figures.

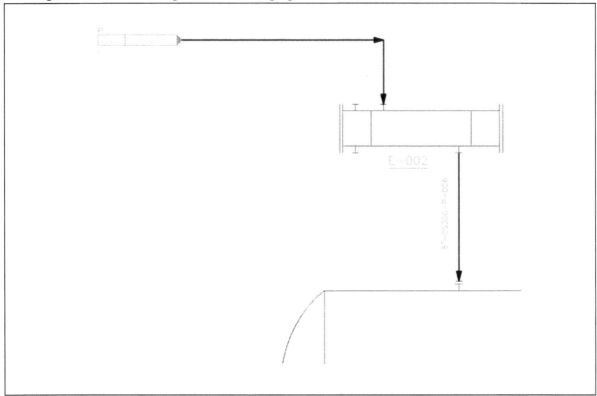

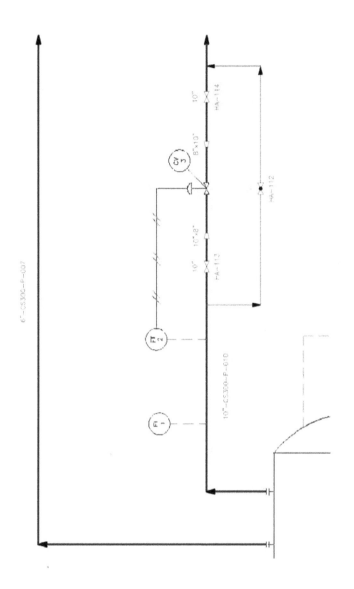

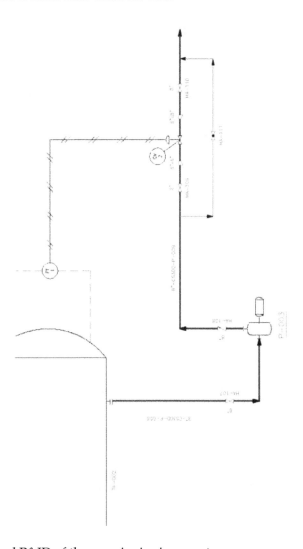

The final P&ID of the exercise is given next.

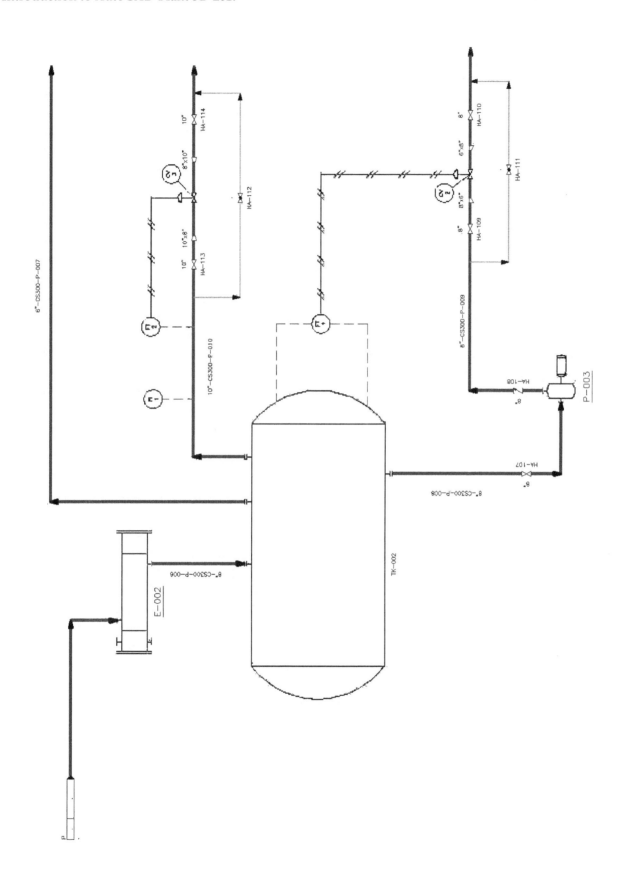

Tutorial 3 (Editing the P&ID)

In this tutorial, you open the drawing created in **Tutorial 1** and modify it.

1. Right-click on **Tutorial1** in the **Project Manager** and select **Open** from the shortcut menu.

Applying Corners

1. To apply corners to a line, select the line connecting the bottom portion of the vessel.

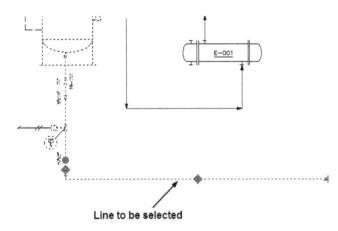

Line to be selected

2. Right-click and select **Schematic Line Edit > Apply Corner**.

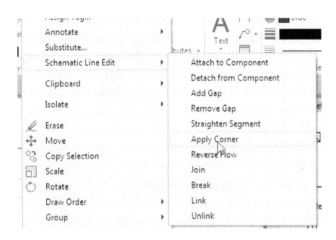

3. Select a point on the line to specify the corner point.

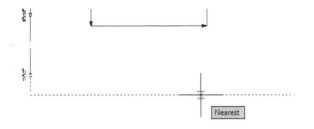

4. Move the pointer downward and click to specify the second point.

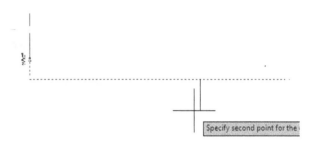

5. Select a point on the line to specify the side of the corner.

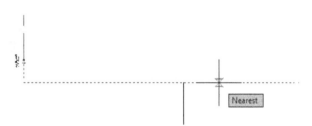

The corner is applied to the line.

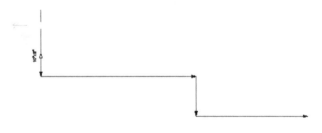

Adding Gaps to lines

In this section, you add gaps to lines. Before adding gaps, you need to create lines passing over equipment.

1. Create two lines passing through the heat exchanger, as shown.

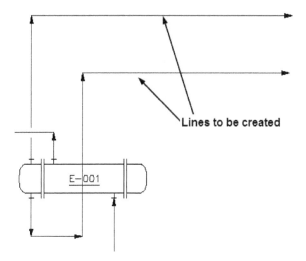

Lines to be created

2. Click the **Edit** button on the **Schematic Lines** panel of the **Home** ribbon.

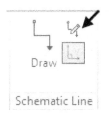

3. Select the line passing over the heat exchanger.

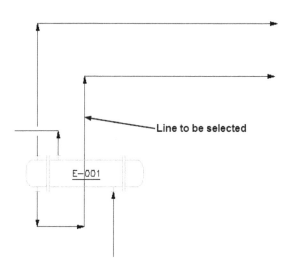

Line to be selected

4. Select the **Gap** option.

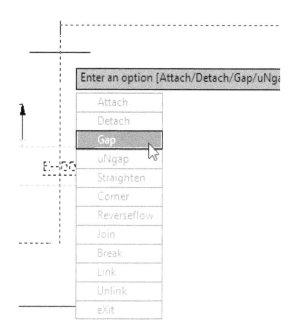

5. Select the first point of the gap.

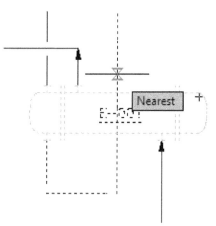

6. Select the second point of the gap.

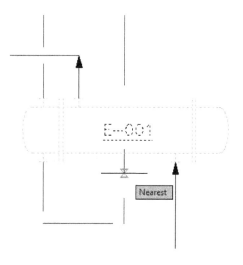

7. Press **Enter** key to create a gap.

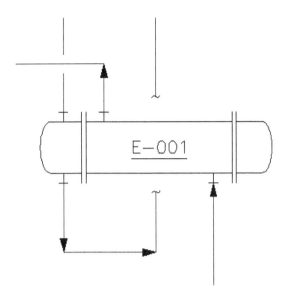

Reversing the Flow Direction

Sometimes you may create a line with wrong flow direction. For example, the line connecting the heat exchanger is created in the opposite flow direction, see figure below.

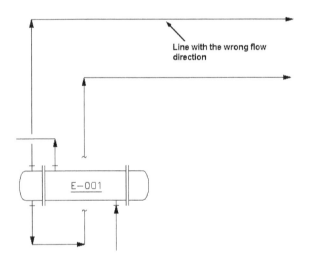

1. Right click on the line, and select **Schematic Line Edit > Reverse Flow**.

The flow direction of the line is reversed.

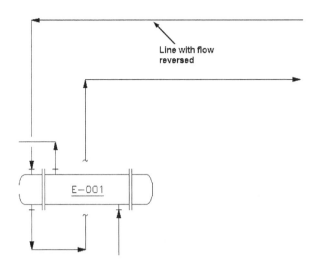

Modifying the lines using grips

In AutoCAD P&ID, you can modify a line using the grips displayed on it.

1. To modify the line using grips, select the line; the Move Schematic line grips appear at the midpoints of the line.

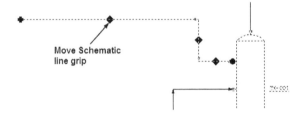

2. Select the **Move Schematic line** grip and move the line downwards.

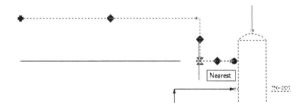

3. Select a point in line to the nozzle. The line is modified.

4. To disconnect the line from a P&ID component, select the Connection point grip displayed on the line and move the pointer away from the

component. The line is detached from the component.

To reattach the line to the component, click on the **Continue grip** and connect it to the component.

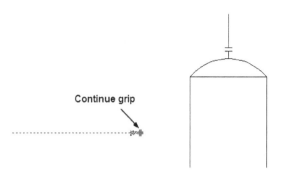

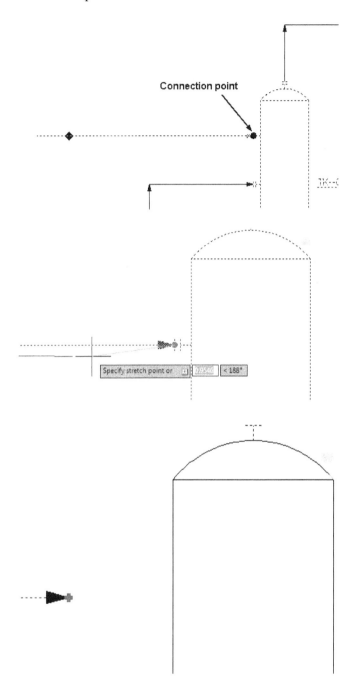

You can also attach a line to the component by right clicking and selecting **Schematic Line Edit > Attach to Component**.

Substituting the Symbols

In AutoCAD P&ID, you can replace symbols by substituting them with another symbol of the same group.

1. To substitute a valve symbol, select the **Check valve** placed on the line connecting the centrifugal pump. The Substitute grip appears on it.

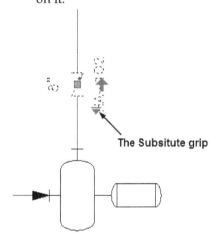

Note: You can also detach a line from a component by using the **Detach** option. To do so, right-click on the line and select **Schematic Line Edit > Detach from component**. Next, specify the end point of the line.

2. Click on the substitute grip to display various valve symbols.
3. Select the Globe Valve.

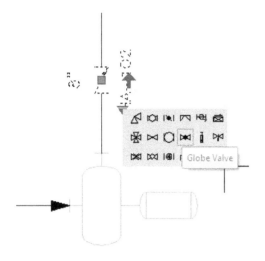

The Globe valve replaces the Check Valve.

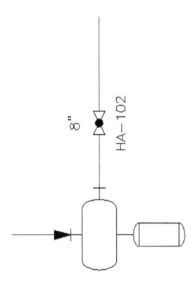

Substituting Instrument symbols

1. To substitute an instrument symbol, select the Temperature Indicator symbol connected to the vessel.

2. Click the Substitute grip.

3. Select **Primary Accessible DCS**.

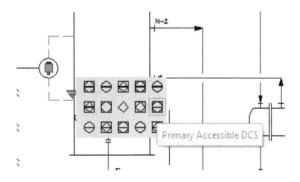

The instrument symbol is replaced.

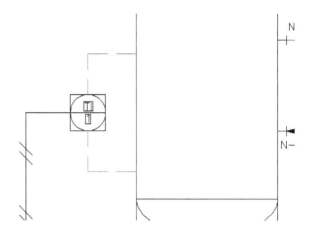

You can also substitute equipment symbols. However, you have to reconnect the pipelines after substituting. For example, on substituting a centrifugal pump with a vertical inline pump, the pipeline is disconnected. You need to connect the pipelines using the grips.

4. Save the P&ID drawing. Do not close it.

Tutorial 4 (Managing Data)

In this tutorial, you learn to view, export and import P&ID data. You need to use the Data Manager to view, export or import data.

1. To Open the Data Manager, click the **Data Manager** button on **Project** panel of the **Home** ribbon.

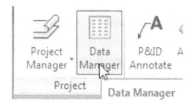

The **Data Manager** appears as shown next. Various components of the **Data Manager** are shown in the figure.

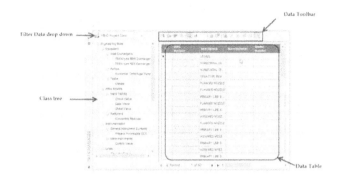

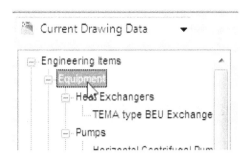

The **Filter Data** drop-down is used to select the type of data to be displayed in the **Data Manager**. You can select the **Current Drawing Data**, **P&ID Project Data** or the **Project Reports.**

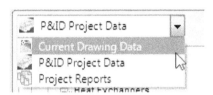

The **Class** tree is used to select the required P&ID class. The data related to the selected type is displayed.

The **Data Manager** toolbar is used to perform various operations such as import, export, view data and so on.

The **Data** table is similar to a spreadsheet and displays data.

Filtering the Data

1. Open the **Tutorial1.dwg**, if not already opened.

2. Open the **Data Manager** by clicking the **Data Manager** button on the **Project** panel.

3. Click **Current Drawing Data** on the **Filter data** drop-down to view the data of the currently opened drawing file.

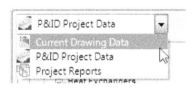

4. Click **Equipment** from the **Class** tree to view all the equipment in the drawing,

5. Click **Nozzles** in the **Class** tree to view the nozzle data

The nozzle data appear in the Data table.

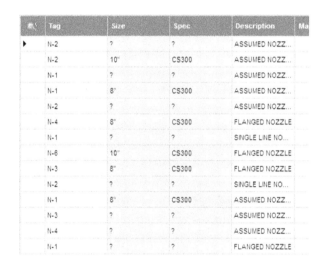

6. To filter the data, right-click on the **8"** size in the **Size** column and select **Filter By Selection**.

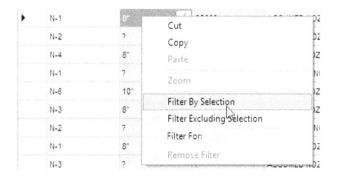

The nozzle data is filtered, and the Data table displays only the 8" size nozzles.

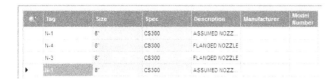

7. To remove the filter, right-click in the **Data** table and select **Remove Filter**.

8. To filter by excluding the selection, right-click on the cell with '**?**' value and select **Filter Excluding Selection**.

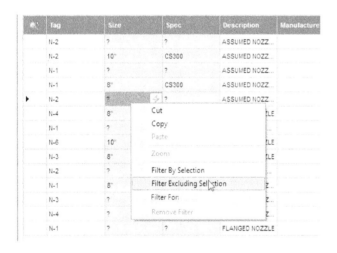

Now, you need to add some information to the Data table.

9. Add the manufacturer information in the **Manufacturer** column.

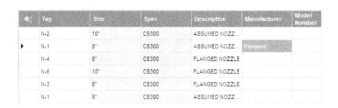

10. Hide the empty columns by clicking the **Hide Blank Columns** button on the **Data Manager** toolbar.

Exporting the Data

1. Export the data by clicking the **Export** button on the **Data Manager** toolbar.

The **Export Data** dialog appears.

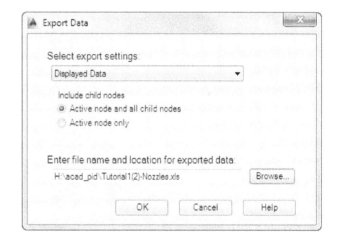

2. Click the **Active node only** option under **Include child nodes**.

3. Click the **Browse** button and specify the location of the export file.

4. In the **Export To** dialog, specify the file type using the **File Type** drop-down.

5. Click the **Save** button

6. Click **OK** to export the data.

7. Browse to the location of the exported file and open it.

8. Enter the **Manufacturer** information.

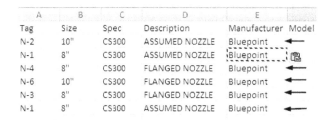

9. Save the spreadsheet.

Now, you need to import the spreadsheet.

10. Click the **Import** button on the **Data Manager** toolbar.

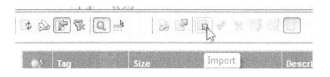

The **AutoCAD Plant** message box appears.

11. Click **OK**.

12. In the **Import From** dialog, browse to the location of the spreadsheet and double-click to open the file. The **Import Data** dialog appears.

13. Click **OK** to import the data.

You notice that all the edited cells are highlighted in yellow color.

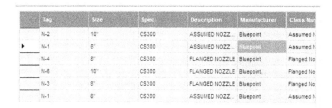

14. Click the fifth row of the first column; the drawing is zoomed to the related nozzle.

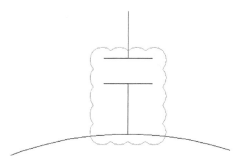

You notice that a revision cloud appears on the nozzle. In addition, revision clouds appear on other modified nozzles.

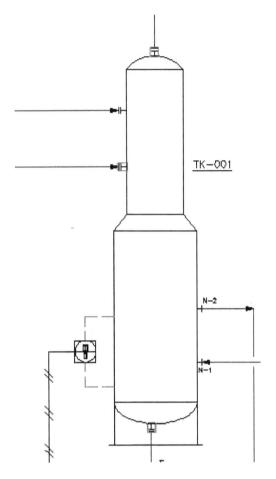

#▷	Tag	Type	Description	Class Name	PnPID
▷	P-001	P	HORIZONTAL CENTRIFU...	Horizontal Centrif...	802
	TK-001	TK	VESSEL	Vessel	675
	P-002	P	HORIZONTAL CENTRIFU...	Horizontal Centrif...	688
	E-001	E	TEMA TYPE BEU EXCHA...	TEMA type BEU E...	1444

3. Drag and place the description below the centrifugal pump.

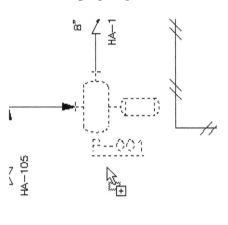

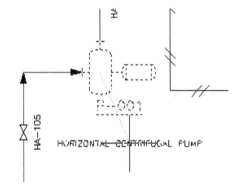

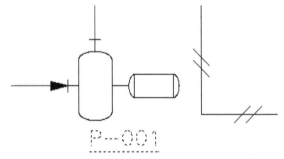

HORIZONTAL CENTRIFUGAL PUMP

15. Click the **Accept** button on the **Data Manager** toolbar to accept the edited value.

16. Click the **Accept All** button to accept all the edited values.

Adding Annotations using the Data Manager

1. Click **Equipment** in the **Class** tree to display the equipment data.

2. In the Data table, click in the **Description** cell of the P-001 component.

Assigning Tags using the Data Manager

You can use the Data Manager to assign tags to the P&ID components.

1. Make sure that the Tutorial 1 file is open.
2. On the Data Manager, click the **Engineering Items > Nozzles > Assumed Nozzle**. You notice

that many nozzles have same tag information. Now, you need to assign a unique tag to each nozzle.

3. Click **Engineering Items > Nozzles > Flanged Nozzle**. You notice that tag information for nozzle N-1 to N-6 is already defined.

4. Click **Nozzles > Assumed Nozzle**.

5. Double-click in the N-1 cell in the **Tag** column.

	Tag	Size	Spec	Description
▶	N-1	4"	CS300	ASSUMED NOZZ...
	N-1	4"	CS300	ASSUMED NOZZ...
	N-2	6"	CS300	ASSUMED NOZZ...
	N-2	6"	CS300	ASSUMED NOZZ...
	N-1	6"	CS300	ASSUMED NOZZ...
	N-2	4"	CS300	ASSUMED NOZZ...
	N-3	?	?	ASSUMED NOZZ...
	N-4	?	?	ASSUMED NOZZ...

6. On the **Assign Tag** dialog, check the Parent Equipment. It shows P-001 which is the centrifugal pump.

7. Type-in 7 in the **Number** box and click **Assign**.

8. Likewise, assign tags to other nozzles, as shown.

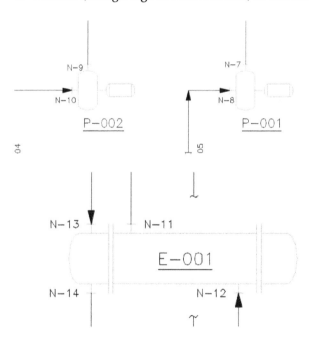

9. Save and close all the files.

Tutorial 5 (Defining a new Class)

In this tutorial, you create a block of a symbol and add it to the category list of the project.

1. Start a new drawing by clicking the **New** button on the Quick Access toolbar.

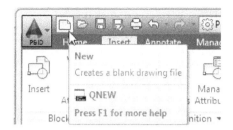

2. Create the symbol shown.

3. Select all the entities of the symbol.

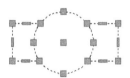

4. Click the **Create Block** button on the **Block Definition** panel of the **Insert** tab.

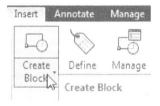

5. In the **Block Definition** dialog, enter **Vacuum Pump** in the **Name** edit box.

6. Click the **Pick Point** button on the **Block Definition** dialog.

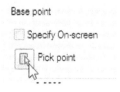

7. Select the center point of the circle as a base point.

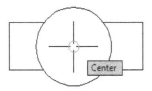

8. Click the **OK** button to create a block.

9. Save the file with the name *Vaccum_Pump.dwg* in the **TUTORIAL PROJECT** folder.

Next, you need to define a new class using the **Project Setup** dialog.

10. Open the **TUTORIAL PROJECT** project, if not already opened.

11. To open a project, click the **Open** option on the drop-down in the **Project Manager**.

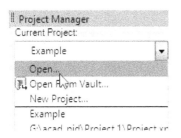

Browse to the **TUTORIAL PROJECT** folder and double-click on the **Project.xml** file.

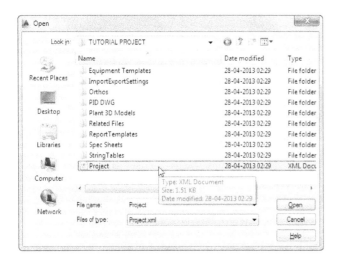

12. Click the **Project Setup** button from the **Project** drop-down in the **Project** panel.

The **Project Setup** dialog appears.

13. Expand the **P&ID DWG Settings** node.

14. In the **P&ID DWG Settings**, expand **P&ID Class Definitions > Engineering Items > Equipment > Pumps**.

15. Right-click on **Pumps** and click **New**.

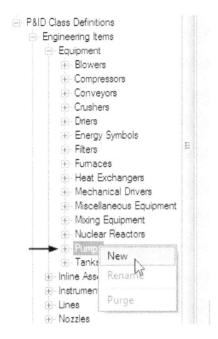

16. In the **Create Class** dialog, enter **Vacuum_Pump** in the **Class Name** field.

17. Type **Vacuum Pump** in the **Display Name of the Class** field.

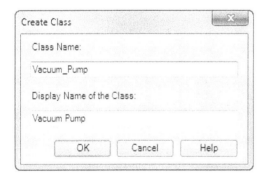

18. Click the **OK** button.

The new class is displayed under the **Pumps** list.

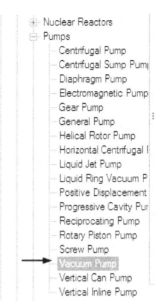

19. Select the **Vacuum Pump** class from the list and click the **Add Symbols** button under **Class Settings: Vacuum Pump**.

The **Add Symbols** dialog appears.

20. In this dialog, click the **Browse** button next to the **Selected Drawings** field.

21. In the **Select Block Drawing** dialog, browse to the **TUTORIAL PROJECT** folder and double-click on the **Vacuum_Pump.dwg**.

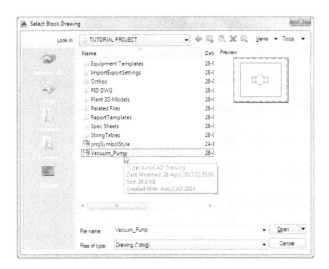

22. In the **Add Symbols** dialog, select **Vacuum_Pump** from the **Available Blocks** list and click the **Add** button.

23. Click the **Next** button.

The **Add Symbols-Edit Symbol Settings** dialog appears.

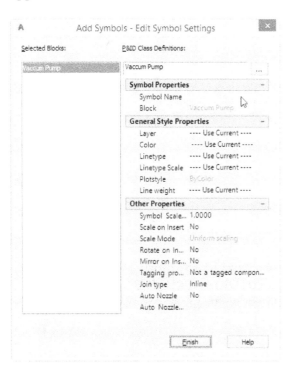

24. Type **Vacuum Pump** in the **Symbol Name** edit box.

25. Specify the other properties, as shown.

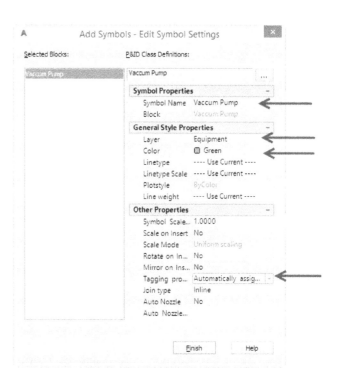

26. Click the **Finish** button to add the symbol to the list.

27. Click the **Edit Block** button under **Class settings: Vacuum Pump**.

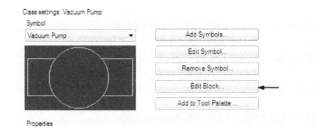

The block editor is opened.

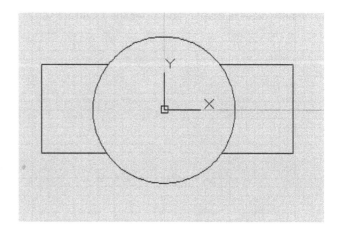

28. Select the **Parameters** tab from the **Block Authoring Palettes** tool palette.

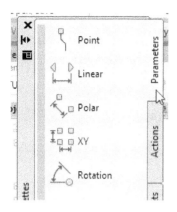

29. Select the **Point** button from the tool palette

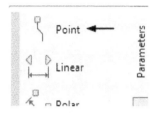

30. Press and hold the **Shift** key and right-click to display the shortcut menu.

31. Click **Midpoint** on the shortcut menu.

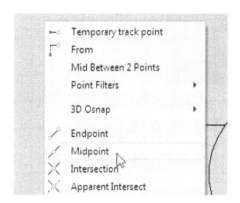

32. Select the midpoint of the left vertical line.

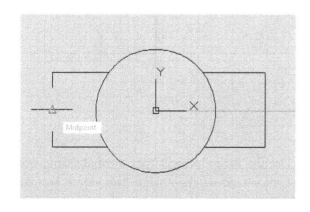

33. Move the pointer toward left and click.

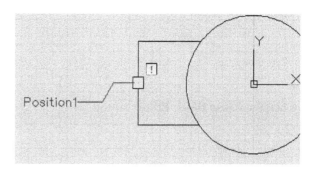

34. Likewise, add another point on the right vertical line.

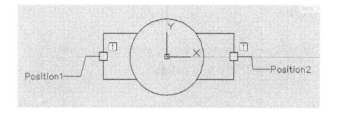

35. Click on the yellow grip displayed on the left point, right click, and select **Properties**; the **Properties** palette is opened.

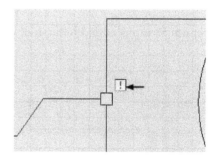

36. In the **Properties** palette, under the **Property Labels**, enter **AttachmentPoint1** in the **Position name** field.

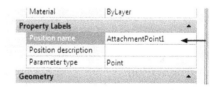

37. Likewise, specify the **Position name** of the second point as **AttachmentPoint2**.

38. Click the **Save Block** button on the **Open/Save** panel.

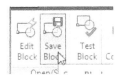

39. Click the **Close Block Editor** button.

Next, you need to add this symbol to the tool palette.

40. Make sure that the **Equipment** tab is opened in the P&ID PIP tool palettes.

41. Click the **Add to Tool Palette** button under **Class Settings: Vacuum Pump** in the **Project Setup** dialog.

42. Click **OK**.

The **Vacuum Pump** is added to the tool palette.

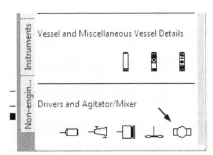

Adding Annotations to the Symbol

Now, you need to add annotations to the symbol

1. To add annotations to the symbol, make sure that **Equipment tag** is selected in the drop-down available under **Annotation**.

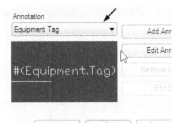

2. Click the **Add Annotation** button under **Annotation** on the **Project Setup** dialog; the **Symbol Settings** dialog appears.

3. Enter **New Equipment tag** in the **Symbol Name** field under the **Symbol Properties** group.

4. Make sure that **Equipment Tag_block** is displayed in the **Block** field.

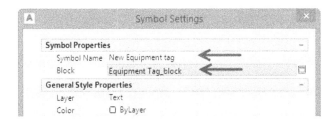

5. Click **OK**.

Now you need to assign a format to the annotation.

6. Click the **Edit Block** button under **Annotation** on the **Project Setup** dialog.

The **Block Editor** is opened.

7. Click the **Assign Format** button on the **Annotation** toolbar.

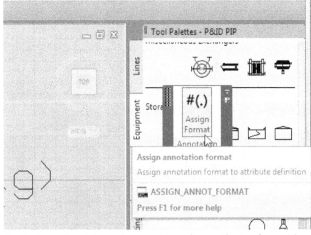

8. Select the **#(Equipment Tag)** attribute from the graphics window; the **Assign Annotation Format** dialog appears.

9. Click the **Select Class Properties** button on the **Assign Annotation Format** dialog.

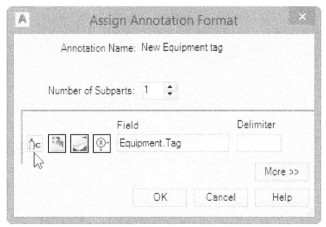

The **Select Class Property** dialog appears.

10. In the **Select Class Property** dialog, select **Engineering Items > Equipment**.

11. Select **Equipment Spec** from the **Property** list.

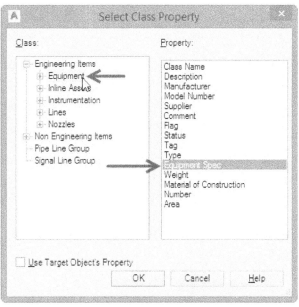

12. Click **OK** on the **Select Class Property** dialog.
13. Click **OK** on the **Assign Annotation Format** dialog.
14. Close the **Block Editor** and save the changes made.

15. In the **Project Setup** dialog, make sure that **Vacuum Pump** is selected in the **Category** list.

16. Set **New Equipment Tag** as the **Default Value** for the **AnnotationStyleName**.

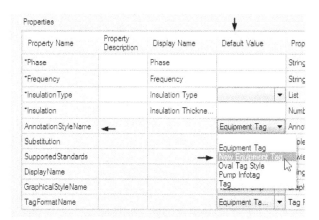

17. Click the **Apply** button.

18. Click the **OK** button.

Tutorial 6 (Generate Reports)

In this tutorial, you generate reports using the Report Creator.

1. Type report in the search bar located on the left side of the taskbar, if you are working in Windows 10.

2. Select Autodesk AutoCAD Plant Report Creator 2017 – English from the search results.

The **Settings** dialog appears.

In this dialog, you can define the location of the report data. You can use the **General** option to define the default location. The **Project** option is used to define the report file location in the **ReportFiles** folder under the current project directory. You can also use the **Custom Path** option to define the custom location for the report files.

3. Select the **General** option from the **Settings** dialog and click **OK**.

4. Click the **Open** option on the **Project** drop-down in the **Autodesk AutoCAD Plant Report Creator**.

5. Browse to location ....**TUTORIAL PROJECT\Project.xml**.

6. Click the **Open** button to the set the project for generating the reports.

7. Select **Linelist** from the **Report Configuration** drop-down.

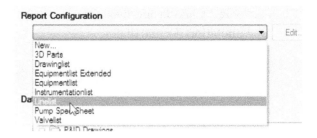

8. Click the **Preview** button; the **Preview** window appears.

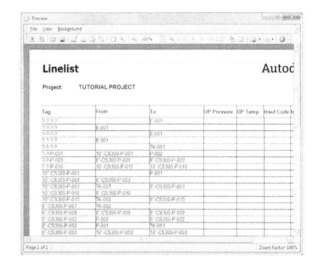

Using the options in this window, you can modify the display of the report by changing the background color, page setup and so on. You can also specify the export format of the report.

You can also save the changes as a template. Click **Export Document > PDF File** on the Toolbar; the **PDF Export Options** dialog appears. Click the **OK** button; the **Save As** dialog appears. Specify the location of the template file.

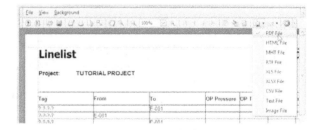

9. Close the **Preview** window.

10. Click **Print/Export**; the **PDF Export Options** dialog appears.

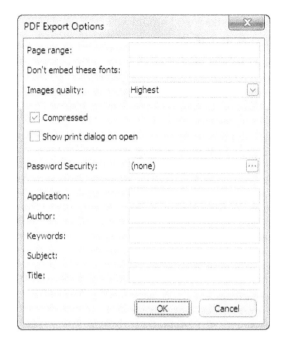

10. Close all the files.

11. Click the **OK** button; the **Export Results** dialog appears.

12. Double-click on the listed PDF file in the **Export results** dialog; the PDF file is opened.

13. View the report in a PDF file.

Linelist

Project: TUTORIAL PROJECT

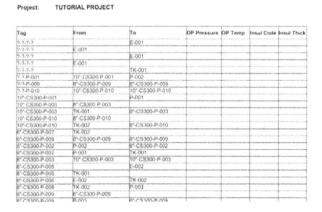

Creating Plant 3D Model

In AutoCAD Plant 3D, you can use the information from the P&ID to create 3D model. The 3D model can be used to visualize a plant. Using the 3D model, you can create orthographic views, section, elevations, and isometric drawings. These drawings are updated when you modify the 3D model.

In this book, you use the Tutorial 1 P&ID to create a 3D model. The steps to create a 3D model in plant 3D are given below:

- Create structural Model

- Create Equipment

- Create piping

- Create inline assets and pipe supports

Creating a Plant 3D Drawing

1. Activate the Tutorial Project using the drop-down located on the **Project Manager**.
2. Click the right mouse button on the **Plant 3D Drawings** folder and select **New Drawing**.

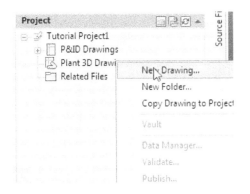

3. On the **New DWG** dialog, type-in **Master Model** in the **File name** box and click **OK**.
4. In the graphics windows, click on the **In-canvas tools** located the top left corner and select **SW Isometric**.

Tutorial 7 (Creating Structural Model)

AutoCAD Plant 3D provides a set of commands to create a structural model. These commands are available on the Structure tab of the ribbon. You can

then use this structural model as a reference to design the plant model. If you want more complex structural model, you can create them in other applications such as Autodesk Revit and AutoCAD Architecture and import them.

Creating Layers

AutoCAD provides you with a feature called layers, which help you to arrange objects. You can learn about layers from the Help file. In this book, you will create layers and use them to arrange different objects of a plant 3D model.

1. On the ribbon, click **Structure > Layers > Layer Properties** .
2. Click the **New layer** button on the **Layer Properties Manager**. Enter **Grid** in the **Name** field.
3. Click the **Color** swatch of the grid layer; the **Select Color** dialog appears.
4. On the **Select Color** dialog, select the Index color **250**, and then click **OK**.

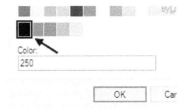

5. Likewise, create other layers, and then assign colors to them, as shown.

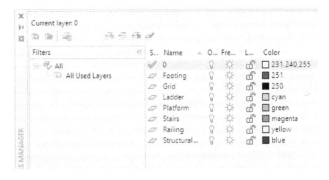

Creating the Grid

1. Change the workspace to **3D Piping**.

2. Change the view orientation to **SW Isometric**.

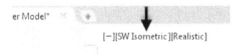

3. On the **Layer Properties Manager**, double click on the Grid layer to set it as current.
4. Close the **Layer Properties Manager** by clicking the **X** (Close) icon at the top left corner.
5. On the ribbon, click **Structure > Parts > Grid**.

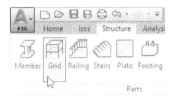

6. On the **Create Grid** dialog, type-in **Platform Grid** in the **Grid name** box. Next, you have to type-in values in the boxes available on the dialog.
7. Click the arrow button next to the **Axis name** box. You notice that the alphabets A, B, C, D are added. These alphabets represent the grid names along the X-axis.
8. Type-in 0, 150, 300, 450 in the **Axis value** box. The values in this box represent the grid spacing along the X-axis. You have to enter values separated by a comma.
9. Click the arrow next to the **Row name** box. The values in the **Row name** box represent the grid names along the Y-axis.

10. Type-in 0, 150, 300 in the **Row value** box. These values define the grid spacing along the Y-axis.
11. Type-in 0,24, 300 in the **Platform value** box. These values define the grid spacing along the Z-axis.
12. Also, enter 0″, +2′, +25′ in the **Platform name** box. They represent the grid names along the Z-axis.

On the dialog, you can type-in a new value in the **Font size** box. The program changes the font size of the grid names.

13. Click **Create** to create a grid.

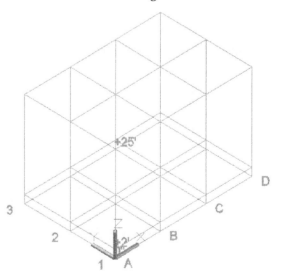

Structural Member Representation

In AutoCAD Plant 3D, you can represent structural members using four different options. You can select these options from the drop-down available on the **Parts** panel.

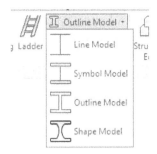

These options are explained in the following illustrations.

Line Model

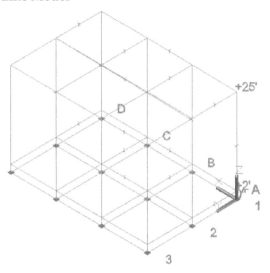

Symbol Model

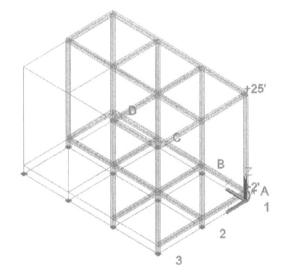

Outline Model

Shape Model

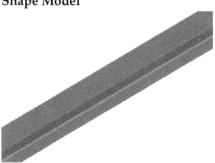

Creating Footings

1. On the Status bar, click the down-arrow next to **Object Snap** icon and select the **Endpoint, Node,** and **Intersection** options. Disable all the other options.

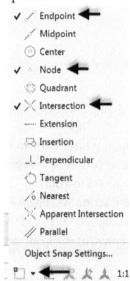

2. On the ribbon, click **Structure > Layers > Layer drop-down > Footing**.

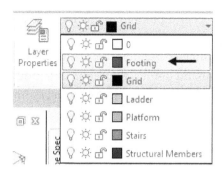

3. On the ribbon, click **Structure > Parts > Footing**.

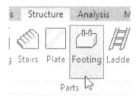

4. Click **Settings** in the command line.
5. On the **Footing Settings** dialog, set the **Standard** to **ASTM** and **Code** to **CONCRETE**.
6. Leave the default dimensions of the footing and click **OK**.
7. Click the lower intersection point of the grid in order to place the footing.

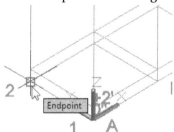

Likewise, place the other footings.

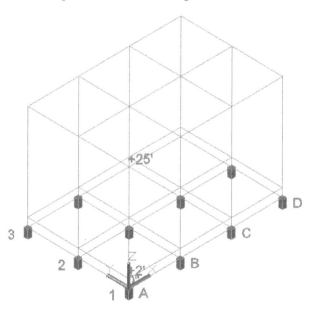

Creating Structural Members

1. On the ribbon, click **Structure > Layers > Layer drop-down > Structural Members**.
2. Activate the Orthomode on the Status bar. Alternatively, press F8 to activate the orthomode.
3. Change the view orientation to **Left**.

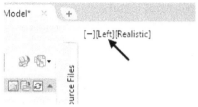

4. On the ribbon, click **Structure > Parts > Member**.

5. Click **Settings** in the command line.

On the **Member Settings** dialog, you can define the parameters of the structural member such as the shape standard, material standard, material code, and shape type and size. You can also set the orientation of the cross-section.

6. Set the **Shape type** to **W** and **Shape Size** to W8X40.
7. Leave the other default values and click **OK**.

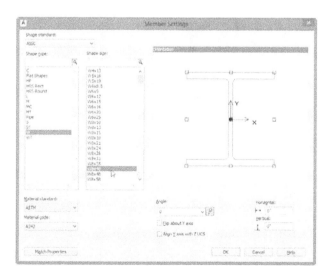

8. Click the lower intersection point of the grid.

9. Move the pointer up and click the intersection point between the vertical and horizontal grid line. The **Member** command creates a vertical structural member. You can select further points to create multiple members.

10. Move the pointer toward right and click the intersection point between the horizontal and vertical grid lines. The command creates a horizontal structural member.

11. Move the pointer down and click the lower intersection point.

12. Press Esc to deactivate the command.

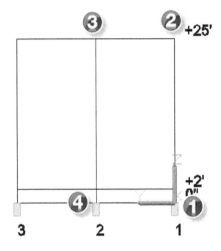

13. Change the view orientation to **SW Isometric**.

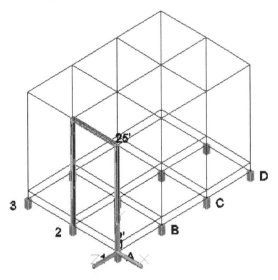

You can create other structure members or copy the existing ones.

14. Select the three structural members, and then click the right mouse button. Select **Copy Selection** from the menu.

15. Select the +25' grid point to define the base point of the copy.

16. Select the intersection points, as shown. The **Copy** command defines the destination points and places copies of the selected objects.

17. Press Esc.

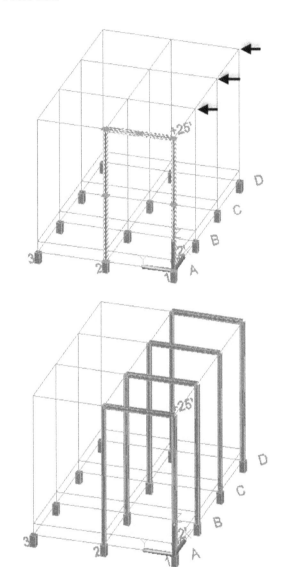

*Note: You can make a selection easily in the **Line Model** representation.*

18. Create other vertical and horizontal structures.

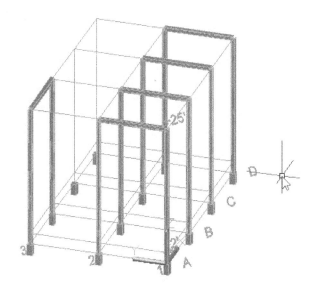

19. Create horizontal structures by selecting the intersections between the gridlines, as shown.

20. Create horizontal structural members by selecting the intersection points between the vertical gridlines and second platform.

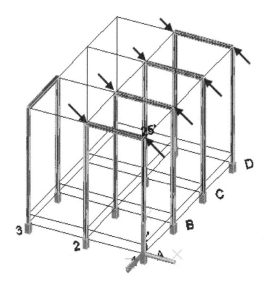

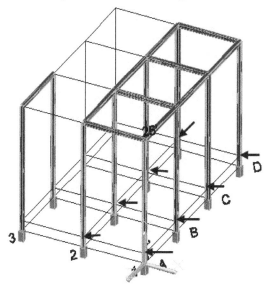

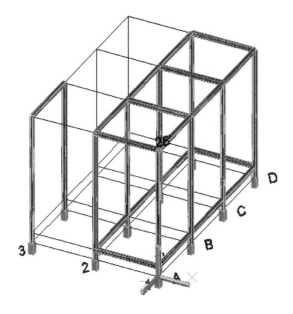

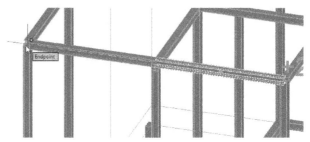

4. Click **Undo** on the **Quick Access toolbar** to restore the structural member to its original length.

5. On the ribbon, click **Structure > Cutting > Lengthen Member**.

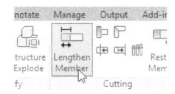

6. Click **Total** in the command line. This option sets a new length of the structural member. The **Delta** option specifies the increase in length of the structural member.
7. Type 25' in the command line and press Enter.
8. Select the horizontal structural member, as shown. The **Lengthen Member** command increases the total length of the member.

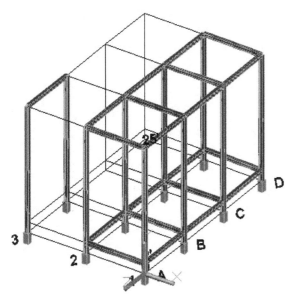

Increasing the length of the Structural Members

1. Click on the horizontal structural member located at the top.
2. Click on the left end grip of the structural member.

3. Move the pointer and click on the grid point, as shown.

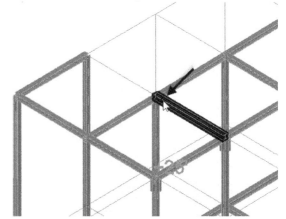

5. On the ribbon, click **Structure > Cutting > Restore Member**.
6. Select the lengthened structural members to restore it to the original length.

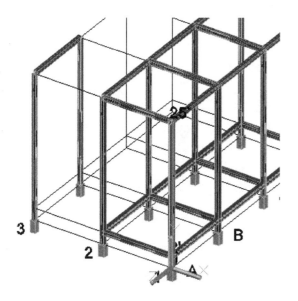

7. Create two horizontal structural members up to the left end.

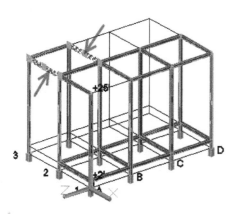

Extending the Structural Members

1. Change the view orientation to **NW Isometric**.
2. On the ribbon, click **Structure > Cutting > Extend Member**.

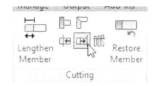

3. On the **Extend to plane** dialog, select **3Points** and click **OK** to define the method to create a boundary plane.
4. Select the grid points, as shown in figure. A boundary plane is set.
5. Select the lower horizontal structural member, as shown in figure. The **Extend Member** command

extends the structural members up to the boundary plane.

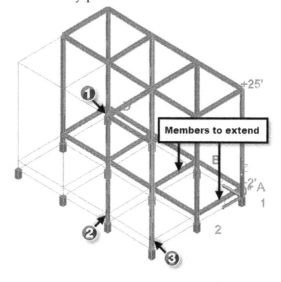

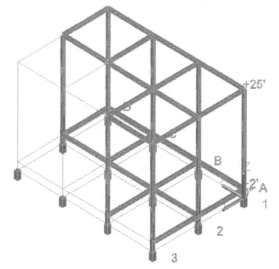

Trimming the Structural Members

1. On the ribbon, click **Structure > Visibility > Hide Others**.

2. Select the structural members and the grid, as shown.

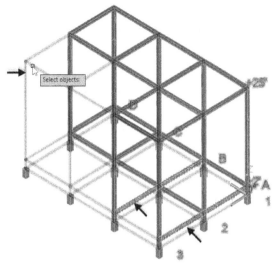

3. Press Enter. All the other objects except the selected ones are hidden.
4. On the ribbon, click **Structure > Cutting > Trim Member** ⊟ .
5. On the **Trim to Plane** dialog, select **3 Points** option and click **OK**.
6. Select the grid intersection points, as shown.
7. Select the portions to trim, as shown. The **Trim Member** command trims the structures by using the intersecting plane created by the three points.

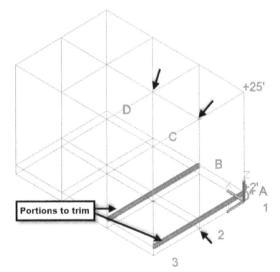

8. On the ribbon, click **Structure > Visibility > Show All** .
9. Change the view orientation to **SW Isometric**.

Using the Cut Back Member command

1. Zoom-In to the intersection between the members, as shown.

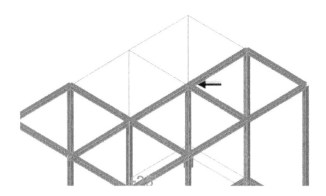

2. On the ribbon, click **Structure > Cutting > Cut Back Member**.

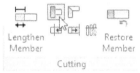

3. Select the limiting member and member to cut. The **Cut Back Member** command cuts the second selection.

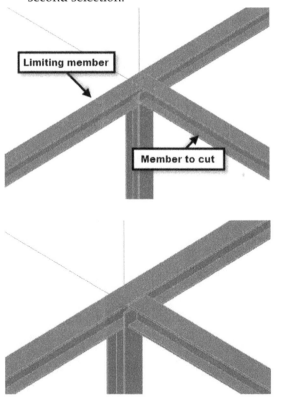

The **cut Both** option in the command line cuts both the members.

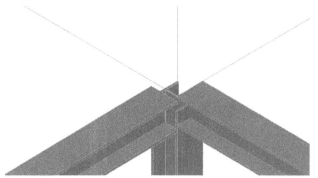

The **Gap** option adds a gap between the two members.

4. Likewise, cut the other members, as shown.

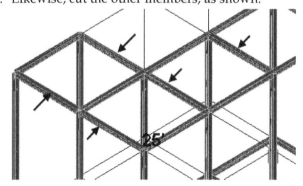

Using the Miter Cut Member command

The **Miter Cut Member** command creates a corner at the intersection point between two structural members.

1. On the ribbon, click **Structure > Cutting > Miter Cut Member**.

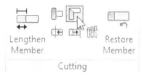

2. Select the two intersecting structural members. The **Miter Cut Member** cuts the structural members to form a corner.

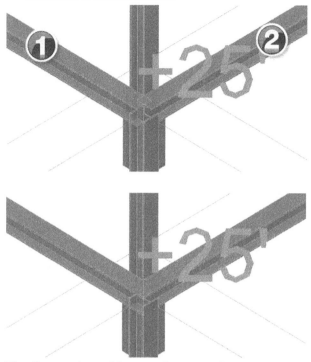

The **Gap** option adds a gap between the two members.

3. Miter the other corners.

Using the Structure Edit command

The **Structure Edit** command edits the structural members, stairs, ladders, grid, footings, and railings.

1. Click on the top horizontal structural members, as shown.

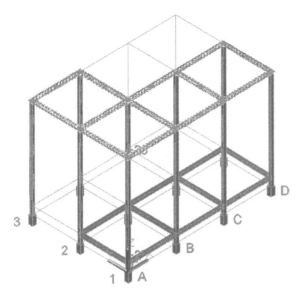

2. On the ribbon, click **Structure > Modify > Structure Edit**.

On the **Edit Member** dialog, you can modify the properties of the structural member. Likewise, if you select any other type of the structural element, the dialog related to it would appear. You can modify the properties on the dialog and click **OK**.

3. On the **Edit Member** dialog, under the **Orientation** section, click the top center point of the cross-section. Click **OK**. The orientation of the structural members is changed to the top center.

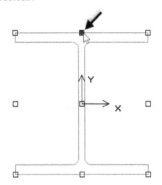

4. Likewise, change the orientation of the structural members on the bottom platform to the top center.
5. Use the **Cut Back Member** command to cut the intersecting portions of the structural members.

Adding Platforms

After creating the structural frame, you have to add platform to accommodate equipment.

1. On the ribbon, click **Structure > Layers > Layer drop-down > Platform**.
2. Click the right mouse button on the grid and select **Isolate > Isolate Objects**. All elements except the grid is hidden.
3. On the ribbon, click **Structure > Parts > Plate**.

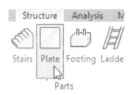

4. On the **Create Plate/Grate** dialog, select **Type > Plate**.
5. Select the **Material Standard** and **Material Code** based on the location of your project.
6. Set the **Thickness** value to 1".
7. Set the **Justification** to **Top**.
8. Set the **Shape** to **New rectangular**.
9. Click **Create** and select the grid points, as shown.

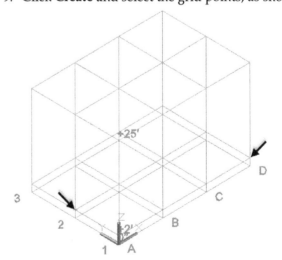

The plate is created.

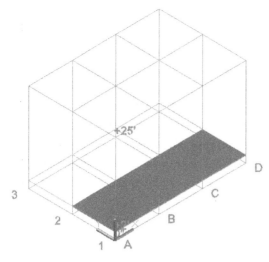

Now, you have to create the top platform.

10. Change the view orientation to top.

11. On the ribbon, click **Structure > Parts > Plate**.
12. On the **Create Plate/Grate** dialog, select **Type > Grating**.
13. Select the **Material Standard** and **Material Code** based on the location of your project.
14. Set the **Thickness** value to 1".
15. Set the **Justification** to **Top**.
16. Set the **Hatch Pattern** to **GRATE**.
17. Set the **Shape** to **New polyline**.
18. Click **Create** and select the grid points, as shown.

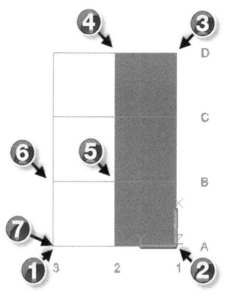

Change the orientation to SW Isometric. You notice that the platform is created at the bottom.

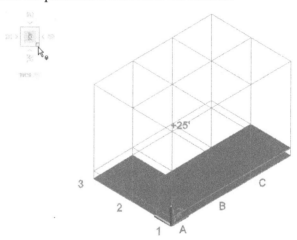

19. Click the right mouse button on the bottom plate and select **Properties**.
20. On the **Properties** palette, scroll down to the **Structural** section. You notice the structural properties of the plate. You can modify these properties.
21. Under the **Geometry** section of the **Properties** palette, click in the **Position Z** box, and then type-in 25'. The bottom plate will be moved to the top.

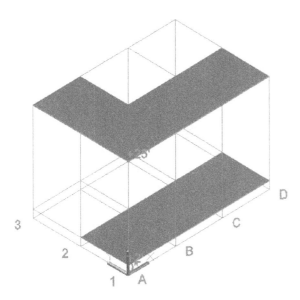

22. Right-click and select **Isolate > End Object Isolation**.

Adding Stairs

1. On the ribbon, click **Structure > Layers > Layer drop-down > Stairs**.
2. Change the view orientation to top.
3. Turn on the Orthomode ⌐ on the status bar.
4. Type-in LINE in the command line and press Enter.
5. Type-in -3',0 in the command line to define the starting point of the line.
6. Move the pointer up and type-in 150 in the command line.

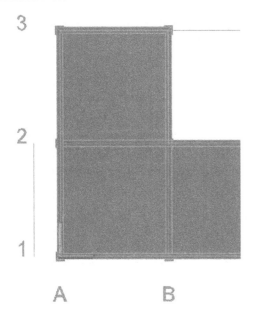

7. Press Esc to deactivate the **Line** command.

8. Change the view orientation to **SW Isometric**.
9. On the ribbon, click **Structure > Parts > Stairs** ✍.
10. Click **Settings** in the command line.

On the **Stair Settings** dialog, the boxes in the Geometry section define the dimensions of the stair set. You can type-in the **Stair width** (inside distance between the stairs) and the **Maximum tread distance** (distance between the steps).

11. Leave the default settings in the **Geometry** section.

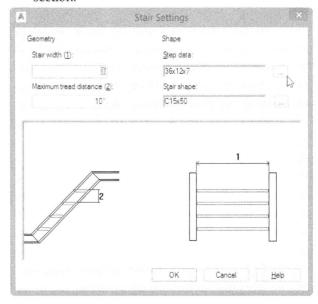

In the **Shape** section, you can define the shape and size of the steps and stairs.

12. To define the step geometry, click the button next to the **Step data** box.

On the **Select Step** dialog, select the **Tread standard** based on the location of the project. You can also select the **User defined** standard. Next, define the dimensions of the tread by selecting already existing configurations from the **Tread shape** section. You can also add a new configuration to this section. To do this, type-in values in the **Dimensions** section, and then click the **Add** button.

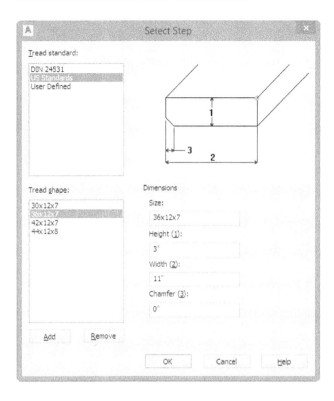

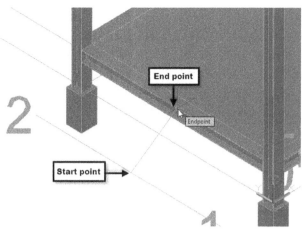

23. Click **OK** on the **Select Step** dialog.
24. Click the button next to the **Stair shape** box.

On the **Select Stair Shape** dialog, you can define the shape standard, shape and size of the stair. Note that you cannot change the orientation and material of the stairs.

30. Press Enter to create the stairs.

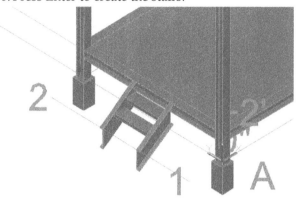

25. Leave the default settings on this dialog and click **Select**.
26. Click **OK** on the **Stair Settings** dialog.
27. On the Status bar, click the down-arrow next to the **Object Snap** icon and select **Midpoint**.

31. Select the stairs, and you notice the grips on it. You can use these grips to modify the stairs.

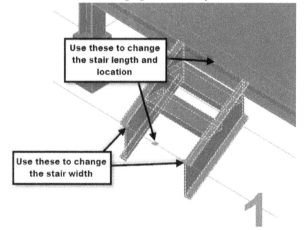

28. Select the midpoint of the line to define the starting point of the stairs.
29. Select the midpoint of the top edge of the platform to define the endpoint of the stair.

You can also use the **Structure Edit** command to modify the stairs.

Adding Railings

1. On the ribbon, click **Structure > Layers > Layer drop-down >Railing**.
2. On the ribbon, click **Structure > Parts > Railing**.
3. Click **Settings** in the command line.

On the **Railing Settings** dialog, the boxes in the **Geometry** section define the distances between the elements of the railing. On the dialog, you can view the image to get a better understanding of these parameters.

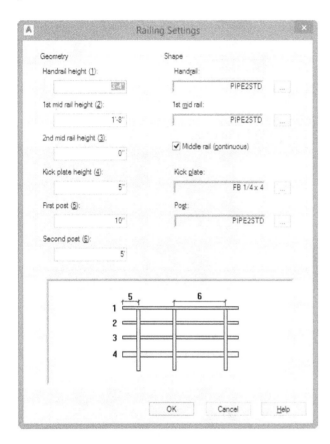

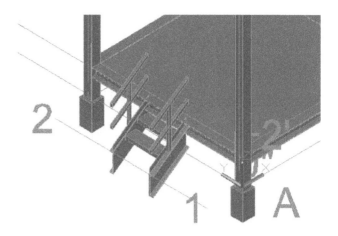

6. Likewise, create railings by selecting the structural members on the top platform.

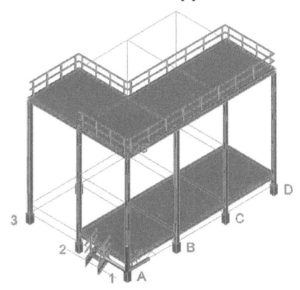

The options in the **Shape** section define the shapes and sizes of the railing elements. For example, to define the shape of the handrail, click the button next to the **Handrail** box. On the **Select Handrail Shape** dialog, select the shape standard, shape, and size. Click **Select** to return to the **Railing Settings** dialog.

4. Leave the default settings on the **Railing Settings** dialog and click **OK**.
5. Click **Object** in the command line and select the stairs. The railing is added to the stairs. You can also add a railing by selecting two points. Click **2Point** in the command line and select start and end points of the railing.

Using the Structure Explode command
This command explodes the grouped structure into individual elements so that they can be modified separately.

1. On the ribbon, click **Structure > Layers > Layer drop-down > Stairs**.
2. On the ribbon, click **Structure > Modify > Structure Explode**.

3. Select the stairs and press Enter. Now, you can select the individual elements of the stairs.
4. On the ribbon, click **Structure > Cutting > Trim Member**.

5. Select **XY WCS** and click **OK**, on the **Trim to Plane** dialog.
6. Select the structural members of the two stairs. The **Trim member** command trims them using the XY plane of the world coordinate system.

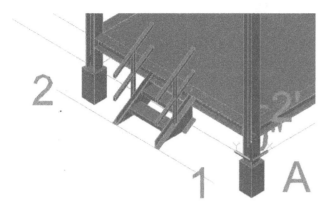

Adding Ladders

1. On the ribbon, click **Structure > Layers > Layer drop-down > Ladder**.
2. On the ribbon, click **Structure > Parts > Line Model**. The model representation changes to line.

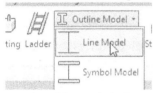

3. On the ribbon, click **Structure > Parts > Ladder** [icon].
4. Click **Settings** in the command line.

On the **Ladder Settings** dialog, the boxes in the **Geometry** section define the dimensions between the ladder elements. The **Width** and **Exit width** boxes define the starting and exit width of the ladder. The **Projection** box determines the extension of the ladder beyond the top point. The **Rung distance** determines the distance between the rungs.

The **Shape** section defines the shapes and sizes of the ladder and rungs. For example, click the button next to the **Ladder Shape** box to change the shape of the ladder. On the **Select Ladder Shape** dialog, define the shape standard, shape and size of the ladder, and then click **Select**.

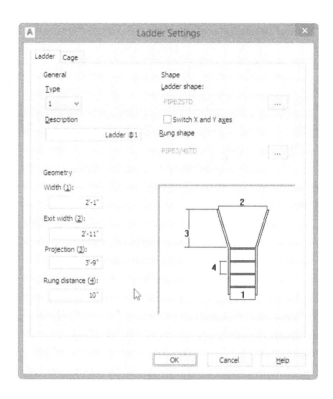

5. Click the **Cage** tab on the **Ladder Settings** dialog.

On the **Cage** tab, check the **Draw Cage** option to create the ladder with a cage. This option avoids the worker from falling.

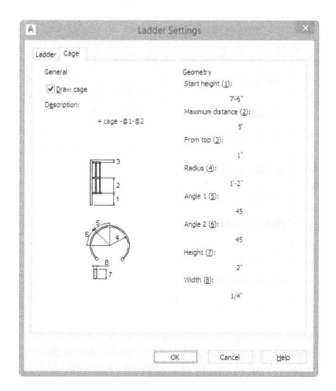

The boxes in the **Geometry** section define the spacing between the cage elements. The **Start height**

box defines the starting point of the cage from the bottom. The **Maximum distance** box determines the distance between the bands. The **From top** box determines the distance between the top ends of the ladder and cage. The **Radius**, **Angle 1**, **Angle 2** boxes define the cage radius, angular locations of the frames on the cage. The **Height** and **Width** boxes define the size of the frames. View the image available on the dialog to understand the parameters.

6. Leave the default options and click **OK**.
7. Activate the **Orthomode** on the status bar.
8. Select the midpoint of the horizontal grid line between 2 and 3.
9. Move the pointer up and choose the midpoint of the top platform.

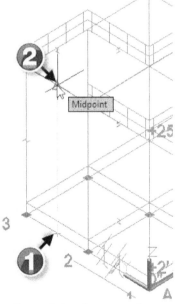

10. Move the pointer downward.
11. Move the pointer horizontally away from the grid up to a small range, and then click. The **Ladder** command creates the ladder at the specified distance from the platform.

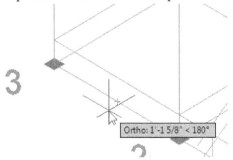

12. Change the structure representation to **Outline Model**.

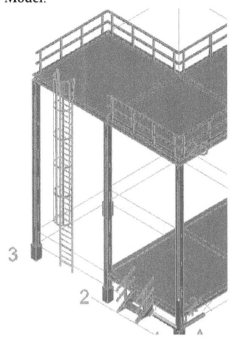

Tutorial 8 (Adding Equipment)

After creating the structural model, you can add process equipment. The equipment you add in a 3D model is always linked with its corresponding symbol in the P&ID. To understand this better, you need to open the **Project Setup** dialog and view which P&ID symbol is mapped to Plant 3D equipment.

1. On the ribbon, click **Home > Project > Project Manager > Project Setup**.

2. On the **Project Setup** dialog, select **Plant 3D DWG Settings > P&ID Object Mapping**.
3. Under the **P&ID Classes** section, click **Engineering Items >Equipment > Pumps >**

Centrifugal Pump. The **Plant 3D Classes** section shows the 3D equipment mapped to the selected symbol.

4. Click **Plant 3D Class Definitions > Piping and Equipment > Equipment > Pump**.

You notice the properties of the pump. Usually, most of the pump properties available in the **Property Mapping** section are linked to the properties of the pump symbols in the P&ID. For example, the **Manufacturer** property of the plant object is same as that in the P&ID.

5. On the **Project Setup** dialog, select **Plant 3D DWG Settings > P&ID Object Mapping**.
6. Under the P&ID Classes section, select **Engineering Items > Equipment > Pumps > Centrifugal Pump**.

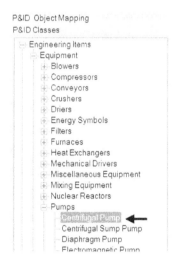

7. Select **Pump** from the **Plant 3D Class Mappings** section and click **Edit** to change the 3D model that is mapped to it. The **Select Plant 3D Class Mapping** dialog appears. On this dialog, you can control the symbols to which the 3D equipment is mapped.

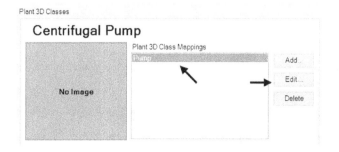

8. Click **Cancel** on the **Select Plant 3D Class Mapping** dialog.
9. Close the **Project Setup** dialog.

Now, you need to place the pumps on the lower platform. Since the platform is at the 2'elevation, you need to create new UCS at this elevation.

10. Select the UCS (User Coordinate System) and click on its origin point.

11. Move the pointer upward and type-in 2'. Press Enter to create a new User Coordinate System.

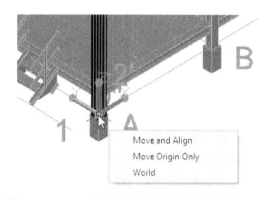

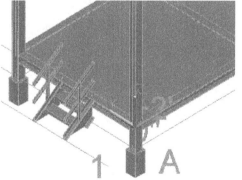

12. Select **Symbol Model** from the Structural Representation drop-down on the Parts panel of the Structure ribbon tab.
13. Change the view orientation to top.

14. On the ribbon, click **Home > Layers > Layers Properties Manager**.

15. On the **Layers Properties Manager**, create a new layer with the name Equipment and change its color to Index color 30.

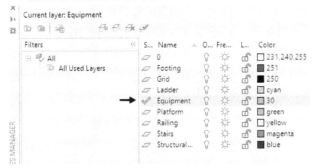

16. Set the Equipment layer as current, and then close the Layers Properties Manager.

17. On the ribbon, click **Home > Equipment > Create**.

18. On the **Create Equipment** dialog, select **Pump > Centrifugal Pump** from the drop-down.

The **Equipment** tab on the dialog has the general information and dimensions of the pump.

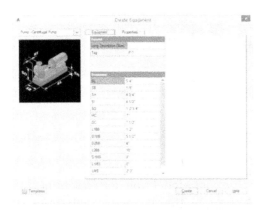

19. Click in the **Tag** box and the **Assign Tag** dialog appears.

20. On the **Assign Tag** dialog, click in the **Number** box and select the button next to it. The number 001 is entered in the box.

21. Click **Assign**. AutoCAD Plant 3D creates a link between this pump and the Centrifugal Pump symbol in the P&ID with P-001 tag.

22. Leave the default dimensions and click the **Properties** tab. The properties of the associated P&ID symbols are populated in this tab. You can also enter a new data to link it to the P&ID symbol.

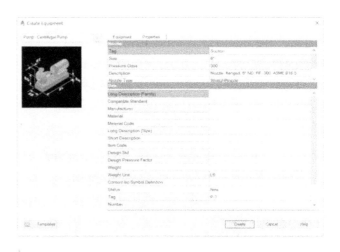

23. Click **Create** on the dialog.

24. Click between A and B, and rotate the pump by 90 degrees, as shown.

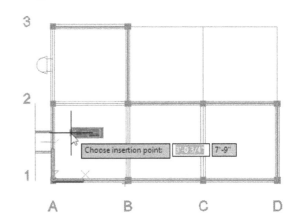

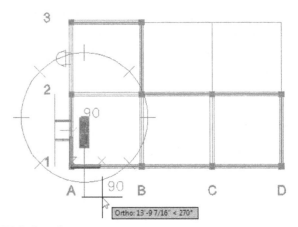

25. Select the pump.

26. On the ribbon, click **Modeling > Modify > Mirror**.

27. Click on the midpoint of the horizontal structural member.
28. Move the pointer downward and click to create the mirror line.

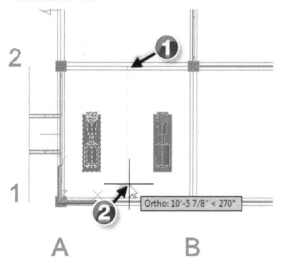

29. Click **No** in the command line.

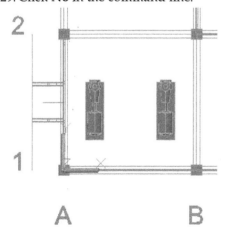

30. On the ribbon, click **Home > Part Insertion > Assign Tag**.

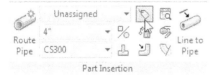

31. Select the mirrored pump to open the **Assign Tag** dialog.
32. On the **Assign Tag** dialog, click in the Number box, and then click the button next to it. The number 002 is entered in it. Click **Assign** to assign a tag. The program associates the mirrored pump with the P&ID symbol with P-002 tag.
33. Activate the **Create Equipment** command.
34. On the **Create Equipment** dialog, select **Vessel > Vertical Vessel** from the drop-down.

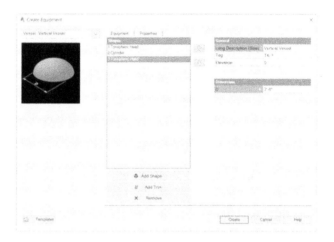

In AutoCAD Plant 3D 2017, the **Add Trim** button is added at the bottom of the **Shapes** list. This helps you to add a saddle, skirt, stiffening ring, lug, platform, leg, flange, and body flange to the vessel.

For example, if you want to add a platform to the vessel, you need to select the shape to which you want to add the platform. Next, click the **Add Trim** button and select **Platform** from the menu. Next, specify the dimensions in the **Dimensions** section of the dialog. You can view the image available on the dialog to get a good idea about the dimensions.

Dimensions	
Platform	^
Platform Shape	Circular ∨
Railing Setup	...
Support Count	2
Support Setup	C4x4.5
A	45
A1	90
A2	45
G	2"
H	4'
W	3'-4"
Ladder	
Create Ladder	Yes ∨
Align to	Platform Right ∨
Ladder Setup	With Cage
G1	7" ∨

35. Click the **Equipment** tab and select **Torispheric Head** under the **Shapes** section.
36. Under **Dimensions**, type-in 7'6"in the **D** box. The **D** box defines the diameter of the Torispheric head.
37. Under **Shapes**, click the **Cylinder** and type-in 7'6"and 25' in the D and H boxes, respectively.
38. Likewise, change the diameter of the bottom **Torispheric Head** to 7'6".
39. Select the Torispheric Head at the bottom of the Shapes section, and then click the Add Trim button.
40. Select **Skirt** from the **Add Trim** menu.
41. Under the **Dimensions** section select **Skirt Type > With Base Ring**.
42. Click in the A1 dimension field and notice the image located on the top left corner of the dialog. The image the explains the A1 and W dimensions.
43. Likewise, refer the image for the remaining dimensions in the Dimensions section.
44. Click in the H field in the Dimensions section and type 6'.
45. Leave the default values in the Dimensions section.
46. Click in the **Tag** box under the **General** section.
47. On the **Assign Tag** dialog, click in the **Number** box, and then click the button next to it. Click **Assign**. The program assigns the tag TK-001 to the vessel.
48. Under **General**, type-in 4' in the **Elevation** box to define the base point of the equipment at an elevation.

49. Click **Create** on the dialog.
50. Click in the space between 3 and 2 grid points.
51. Rotate the vessel by 180 degrees and click.

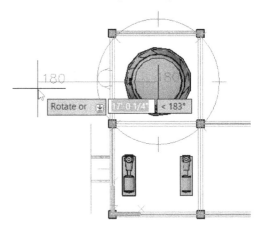

Creating an Equipment using Pre-Defined Shapes

AutoCAD Plant 3D offers you several equipment types. However, sometimes you may want to create equipment, which is not available in the library. In that case, you can use pre-defined shapes such as a rectangle, cylinder, elliptical head, and pyramid and so on to create a new equipment type.

1. Change the view to **SW Isometric**.
2. Select the UCS located on the second platform.
3. Click on the origin of the UCS and move the pointer up.
4. Type-in 25' and press Enter. The UCS is moved to the top platform.
5. Change the view orientation to Top.
6. On the ribbon, click **Home > Equipment > Create**.
7. On the **Create Equipment** dialog, select **Heat Exchanger > New Horizontal Heat Exchanger** from the drop-down. The **Shapes** list appears empty. If not, select the existing shapes and click the **Remove** button.
8. Click the **Add** button and select **2:1 Torispheric Head**.
9. Likewise, add other shapes using the **Add** button.

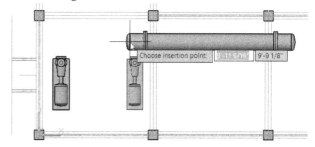

10. Under **Shapes**, click **Torispheric Head** located at the top.
11. Under **Dimensions**, type-in 1'8" in the **D** box. This defines the diameter of the Torispheric head.
12. Under **Shapes**, click the **Cylinder** located at number 2 position.
13. Under **Dimensions**, type-in 1'8" and 17'4" in the **D** and **H** boxes, respectively.
14. Likewise, change the dimensions of other shapes. The dimensions of all the shapes are given below.

Shapes	D	H
Torispheric Head	1'8"	
Cylinder	1'8"	1'8"
Cylinder	1'8"	14'2"
Cylinder	1'8"	1'8"
Torispheric Head	1'8"	

15. Select the **Cylinder** from the **Shapes** list.
16. Click the **Add Trim** button and select **Body Flange** from the menu.

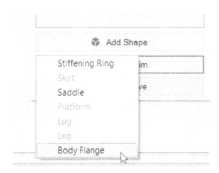

17. In the Dimensions table, set the **Orientation** to **Mating Flange Set**, and then change the H value to 0.

18. Select the **Cylinder** located at the number 4 position in the **Shapes** list.
19. Click the **Add Trim** button and select **Body Flange** from the menu.
20. In the **Dimensions** table, set the **Orientation** to **Mating Flange Set**, and then change the **H** value to 1'8".
21. Select the **Cylinder** located at the number 3 position in the **Shapes** list.
22. Click the **Add Trim** button and select Saddle.
23. In the **Dimensions** table, set the **Orientation** to **Pair**.
24. Change the L and L3 values to 0'8" and 12'6", respectively.
25. Click in the **Tag** box under the **General** section.
26. On the **Assign Tag** dialog, click in the **Number** box, and then click the button next to it. Click **Assign**. The program assigns the tag E-001 to the heat exchanger.
27. Under **General**, type-in 3'4" in the **Elevation** box to define the base point of the equipment at an elevation.
28. Click **Create** on the dialog and position the heat exchanger at the location shown.

29. Type-in 0 as the rotation angle and press Enter.
30. Change the view orientation to **SW Isometric** and **View Style** to **Realistic**.

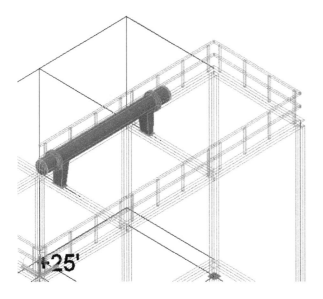

Adding Nozzles

Most of the equipment available in AutoCAD Plant 3D library has nozzles. Nozzles are used to create pipe connections. However, when you create new equipment using predefined shapes, the nozzles are not added to them. You need to add nozzles manually to the equipment.

1. Click on the heat exchanger and the nozzle symbol appears. It is called the **Add Nozzle** tool.
2. Click on the **Add Nozzle** tool. The **Add Nozzle** dialog appears.

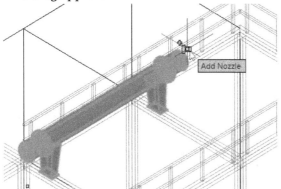

3. On the **Add Nozzle** dialog, click the **Change Type** tab.

On the **Change Type** tab, the top section is used to add nozzle tag. You can enter the type and number values. The entered data is stored in the project database.

There are four nozzle types available on this dialog: **Straight Nozzle, Bent Nozzle, Vent Nozzle,** and **Manway**.

4. Type-in **13** in the **Number** box and click **Close**.

5. Select the **Straight Nozzle** type.
6. Set the **Size, End Type, Unit,** and **Pressure Class** to **4″, FL, in,** and **300**, respectively.
7. Select the RF nozzle from the list.

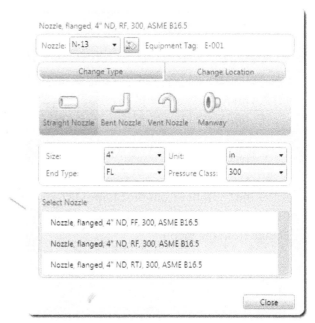

8. Click the **Change Location** tab and select **Nozzle Location > Radial**.
9. Type-in **8″, 90** and **6″** in the **H, A,** and **L** boxes, respectively.
10. Click **Close** and you notice that the nozzle is added to the Heat exchanger.
11. Likewise, add other nozzles to the heat exchanger. The nozzle tags should match the nozzles in the P&ID.

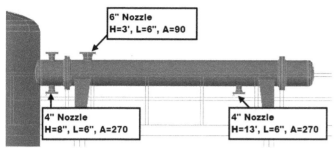

12. On the ribbon, click **Home > Equipment > Modify** and then select the heat exchanger.
13. On the dialog, click the **Templates** button and select **Save current settings as template**. The **Save Template To** dialog appears, and you will be taken to the **Equipment Templates** folder.
14. Type-in *Custom Heat Exchanger* in the **File name** box, and then click **Save**.
15. Click **OK** to close the **Create Equipment** dialog.

Using the Convert Equipment command

In addition to creating equipment using predefined shapes, you can create 3D models using the AutoCAD commands and convert them into equipment.

1. Create a 3D model using the AutoCAD commands. For example, there is a cooler model, as shown.

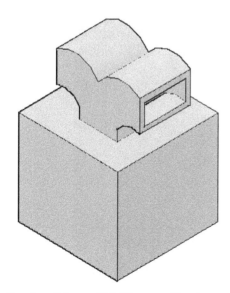

2. On the ribbon, click **Home > Equipment > Convert Equipment**.
3. Select the 3D model and press Enter.

4. On the **Convert to Equipment** dialog, select the equipment type. For this example, just select the **Misc equipment** type.
5. Click **Select**, and then select a point on the 3D model to define the insertion point.
6. On the **Modify Equipment** dialog, enter values in the **Equipment** and **Properties** tabs. You can use the **Templates** button if you want to save this equipment for further use. Click **OK** to close the dialog.

To add nozzles to the equipment, click on it and select the **Add Nozzle** tool. Select a point on the equipment to define the center of the nozzle. Move the pointer and click to define the direction of the nozzle. On the **Add Nozzle** dialog, select the nozzle type and size. Click **Close**.

Modifying Nozzles

The nozzles that are added to the equipment may not be of the required size. You can modify the nozzles to change the size and location.

1. Zoom to the lower portion of the vessel.
2. Ctrl+click the nozzle located on the vessel.
3. Click the **Edit Nozzle** tool (pencil symbol).

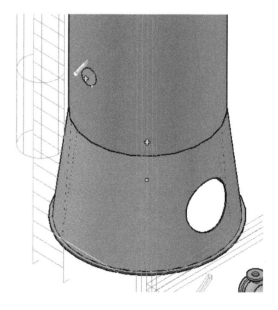

4. On the **Modify Nozzle** dialog, click the **Tag** button to expand the top section.
5. Type-in **4** in the **Number** box. Click **Close** to hide the top portion.

6. Click the **Change Location** tab and type-in 6″ in the **L** box.
7. Type-in 3′9″ in the **H** box.
8. Type-in 90 in the **A** box.
9. Click **Close** on the dialog.

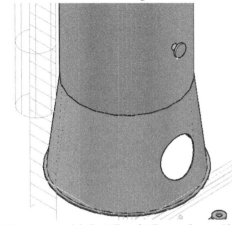

10. Likewise, add the 6″and 4″ nozzles at 8′4″and 5′ heights, respectively. The radial angle is 180 degrees. The nozzle tags should be N-1 and N-2.

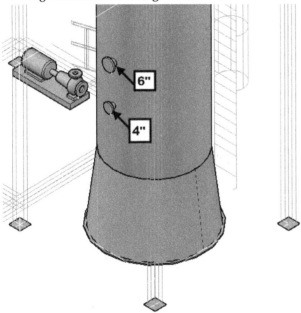

11. Change the nozzle tags of the pumps using the **Modify Nozzle** dialog.

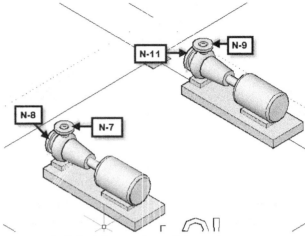

Tutorial 9 (Creating Pipes)

AutoCAD Plant 3D provides various tools and techniques to create piping. In this tutorial, you learn to create piping using these tools and techniques.

Using the Spec Viewer

To create piping in AutoCAD Plant 3D, you need to have a basic understanding about the piping materials. AutoCAD Plant 3D comes with a database of piping components. The information related to the piping components is stored in specifications file. You can access different specifications by using the **Spec Viewer** (on the ribbon, click **Home > Part Insertion > Spec Viewer**).

1. On the **Spec Viewer** palette, select the desired spec from the **Spec** drop-down.

You can view the piping components available in the selected specs under the **Spec Sheet** section. There are different categories of components such as blind flange, bolt set, cap, tees, and valves and so on. Each category has different types of components. For example, scroll down to the **Valve** category to notice that there are different valve types (Ball Valve, Butterfly Valve, Check Valve, Gate Valve, Globe Valve, and Plug Valve) available. These valve types are available in different size ranges.

2. Select the butt weld Ball Valve (**Ball Valve, Long Pattern, 300 LB, BW, ASME B16.10, ASTM A216 Gr WPB, Hand Lever**).

The **Part Sizes** section lists the available sizes. These part sizes are based on the industry standards. You can select a part size and insert into the model.

There are three buttons available on the Spec Viewer. The **Insert in Model** button inserts the selected part size into currently opened AutoCAD Plant 3D file. The **Add to Palette** button adds the selected part size to the Dynamic Tool Palette. The

Create Tool Palette button creates a new Tool Palette from the selected Spec.

Editing Specs

You can edit a Spec using the **Spec Editor** application which comes with AutoCAD Plant 3D.

1. On your desktop, click the **AutoCAD Plant 3D Spec Editor 2017** icon to start this application.

2. On the initial screen, click **Open** and go to C:\ AutoCAD Plant 3D 2017 Content\ CPak ASME.

3. Select the CS300.pspx file and click **Open**. The program opens the CS300 spec file, which is used in this book.

You can also import the specifications files from other software's such as AutoPLANT and CADWorx, and then convert it into AutoCAD Plant 3D format. To do so, click **File > Convert** and select an option from the menu.

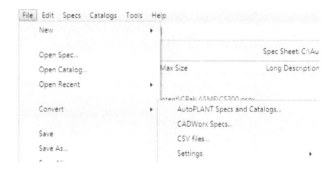

The **Spec Editor** appears similar to the Spec Viewer. It contains all the piping components available in the selected Spec file. In the Spec file, there are many piping components available of same type and sizes. For example, there are two types of Bolt sets under the BoltSet category. In this case, the program shows an error asking you to specify the part to be used first. You need to define the **Part Use Priority** to solve this error.

4. Scroll down to the **Valve** category and click on the error ⬦ symbol in the **Part Use Priority** section of the Check Valve.

5. On the **Part Use Priority** dialog, click 4" from the **Size Conflicts** section.
6. Under the **Spec Part Use Priority** Section, click Gate Valve, Solid Wedge, 300 LB ...
7. Keep clicking the **Up** arrow button to move the gate valve to top.

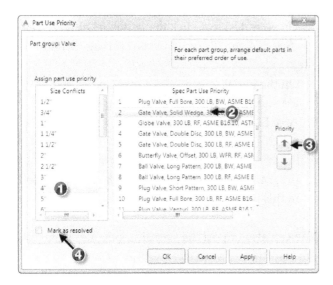

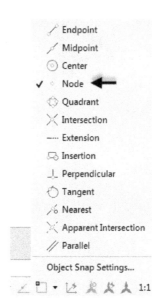

8. Likewise, set the **Part Use Priority** of the 6"valve to Gate Valve, Solid Wedge.
9. Check the **Mark resolved** option.
10. Click **OK**. The error symbols still appear even after you have resolved the part use priority for 4"and 6" only.
11. Save the Spec file, and then close the Spec Editor.

Using P&ID Line Lists to create Piping

AutoCAD Plant 3D allows you to add pipes to a 3D model using different methods. You can just add pipes to a model or use the P&ID Line list. The pipes created using P&ID Line Lists are linked to the P&ID automatically. The P&ID Line list shows all the schematic lines that are created in the project P&ID. Follow the steps given below to create pipes using the P&ID Line List.

1. On the status bar, click the down arrow next to the **Object Snap** icon and make sure that only the **Node** option is selected.

2. On the ribbon, click **Home > Part Insertion > P&ID Line List**.

The P&ID LINE LIST palette appears showing the different line groups.

3. On the P&ID LINE LIST palette, select **Tutorial 1** from the drop-down located at the top.
4. Expand 002 line and select **4"-CS300-P-002**.

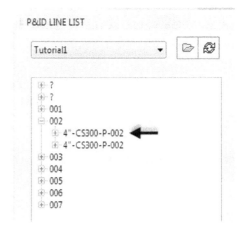

5. Click the **Place** button.
6. Select the discharge nozzle of the left pump.

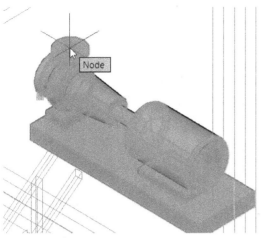

7. Move the pointer up.
8. Click **Plane** in the command line to change the plane in which the pipe is created.
9. Select the node of the nozzle attached to the vessel.

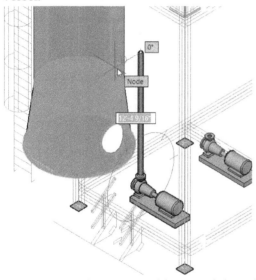

10. Click **Next** in the command line until the solution shown in the figure is displayed.

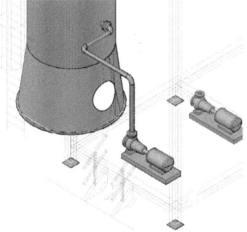

11. Click **Accept** in the command line to accept the solution.

12. Place the pointer on the pipe to view the tag information of the pipe. Now, you cannot assign tag to the pipe as it is linked to P&ID schematic line. Any change in the P&ID tag information is reflected in the pipe, automatically.

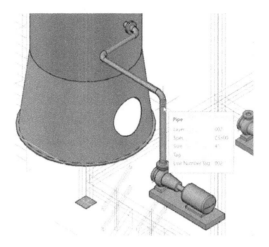

13. On the Status bar, click the down arrow next to the **Object Snap** icon and select the **Nearest** option.
14. On the **P&ID Line List** palette, expand the **4"-CS300-P-002** and select **Check Valve HA-101**.
15. Click **Place** and move the pointer on the horizontal pipe. The check valve is aligned to the pipe.

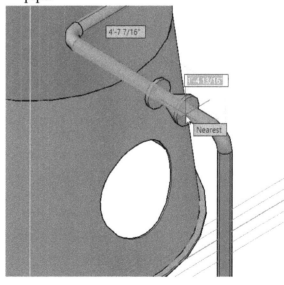

16. Select the endpoint of the pipe to place a check valve.
17. Press **Enter** to use the default rotation angle.

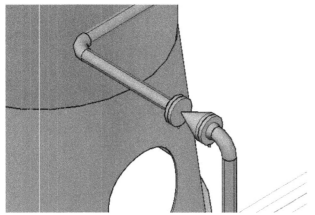

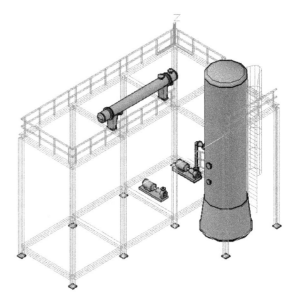

Using the Routing tools to create Pipes

On the **Part Insertion** panel, there are some routing tools (**Route Pipe, Route New Line, Line to Pipe,** and PCF to Pipe) to create pipes.

The **Route New Line** tool helps you to create a pipe by adding a new line number to it. This tool can be useful to create a 3D piping model before creating the P&ID. This tool is available in the **Line Number Selector** drop-down. On this drop-down, the **Show all line numbers** option displays all the available line numbers in the project.

The **Route Pipe** tool creates a new pipe without assigning any tag to it. If you want to create a pipe using a P&ID line number, then select the line from the **Line Number Selector** drop-down and route the pipe.

The **Line to Pipe** tool converts a line or polyline into a pipe.

The **PCF to Pipe** tool creates piping using the **Piping Component File**.

Now, you create pipes using a P&ID Line number.

1. Change the view to NE Isometric.

2. On the **Part Insertion** panel, click **Line Number Selector > Show all line numbers**.
3. Select **006** from the **Line Number Selector** drop-down.
4. Select **6″** from the **Pipe Size Selector** drop-down.
5. Select **CS300** from the **Spec Selector** drop-down to define the pipe spec.

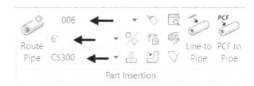

6. On the ribbon, click **Home > Part Insertion** panel **> Route Pipe**.
7. Select the **6″** nozzle attached to the heat exchanger.

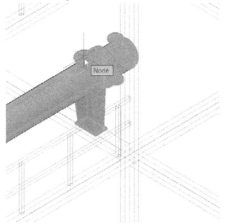

8. Move the pointer along the X-axis and type-in 2′. Press Enter.

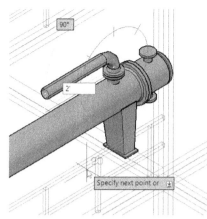

9. Click **Plane** in the command line until the pipe is oriented along the Y-axis.

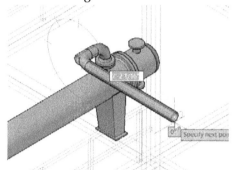

10. Type 4'and press Enter.
11. Zoom to the vertical vessel and select the 6" nozzle attached to it.

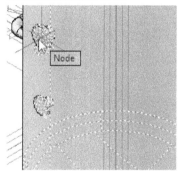

12. Click **Next** in the command line until the solution appears, as shown.

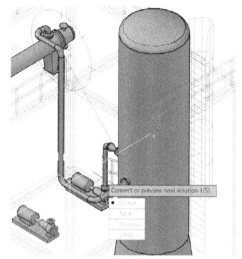

13. Click **Accept** to create the pipes.

A pipe connection is created between the selected nozzles. Place the pointer on the pipe connection and you notice that the tag information of the 006 P&ID schematic line is assigned to it.

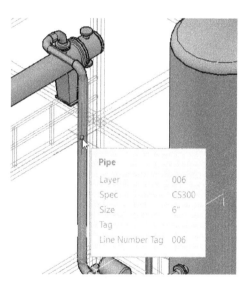

14. On the **Part Insertion** panel, click **Line Number selector > Unassigned**.
15. Change the view orientation to **SW Isometric**.
16. Click on the left pump to highlight it.
17. Zoom to the pump and select the + mark of the 6" nozzle, as shown.

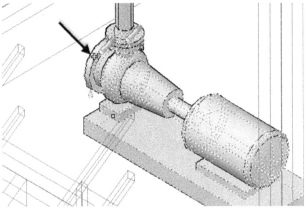

18. Move the pointer rightward and click on the 6"
nozzle of the right pump.

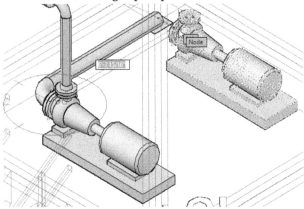

19. Click **Accept** in the command line.

20. Place the pointer on the pipe connection between
the two pumps. You notice that the tag
information is not assigned to the pipe.

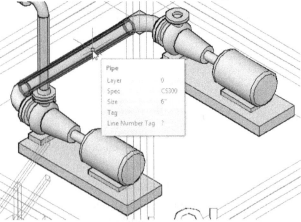

21. Click on the pipe, right click, and then select **Add
to selection > Entire Line number**.

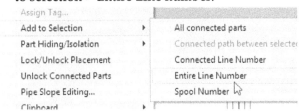

22. Right click and select **Properties**.

23. On the **Properties** palette, scroll down to the **Tag**
section.

24. Under the **Tag** section, click **Line Number >
Show All line numbers**.

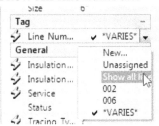

25. Select **Line Number > 007**. The line tag of the 007
P&ID schematic line is assigned to the pipe.

Using the Line to Pipe command to create Pipes

1. On the status bar, activate the **Ortho Mode** icon.

2. On the ribbon, click **Modeling > Draw > 3D
Polyline**.

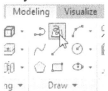

3. Zoom to the heat exchanger and select the node
point of the 4" nozzle.

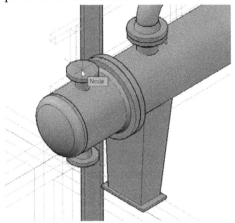

4. Move the pointer up and click to create a vertical
line.

5. Likewise, create horizontal and vertical lines, as
shown.

6. Right click and select **Enter**.

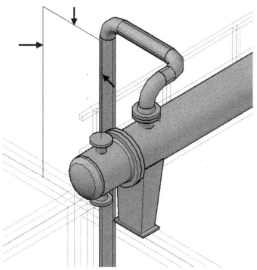

7. On the **Part Insertion** panel of the **Home** tab, select 4" from the **Pipe Size Selector** drop-down.

8. On the **Part Insertion** panel, click the **Line to Pipe** icon.

9. Click on the 3D polyline and press Enter. The line is converted to pipe.

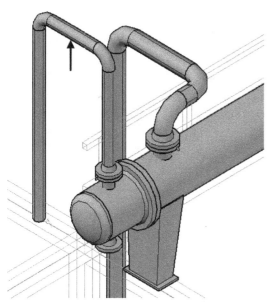

Knowing about the Compass

You may have noticed a red circle with tick marks while routing a pipe. It is called Compass and it can be used to rotate the pipes. The settings related to Compass are available on the **Compass** panel of the ribbon.

The **Toggle Tick Marks** icon hides/shows tick marks on the compass. You can type-in a value in the **Tick Mark Increments** box to define the angle between the tick marks.

The **Toggle Snaps** icon forces the pipe to rotate at the angular increments defined in the **Snap Increments** box.

The **Toggle Tolerance** icon enables the pipe to deflect slightly from the elbow angle. Activate this button and type-in a tolerance angle in the **Tolerance Snap Increment** box. The pipe is allowed to deflect within the specified tolerance angle.

The **Toggle Compass** icon shows/hides the Compass while routing a pipe.

On the expanded **Compass** panel, there are options to change compass color and diameter.

Editing Pipes

The process of editing pipes is similar to that of editing AutoCAD objects. AutoCAD Plant 3D offers various grips that appear when you select a pipe.

1. Zoom to the heat exchanger and select the horizontal portion of the pipe created by converting the 3D polyline.

2. Click on the Move Part grip located at the middle of the horizontal pipe.

3. Move the pipe downward and click to change the height.

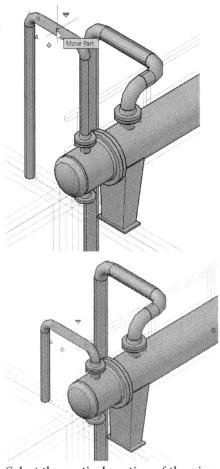

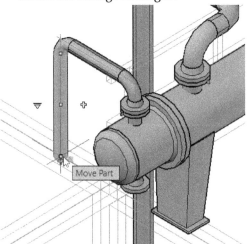

4. Select the vertical portion of the pipe connection, and then click on the Move part grip located at its end.

5. Move the pointer upward and click to reduce the length of the pipe. You can also type-in a value to define the change in length.

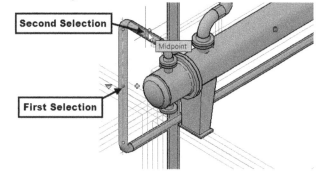

6. Change the view orientation to **Back**.

7. Again, select the vertical portion of the pipe connection.

8. Click on the + mark to activate the PLANTPIPEADD command.

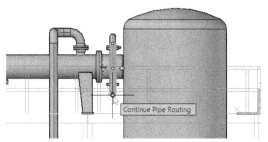

9. Now, continue routing the pipe, as shown.

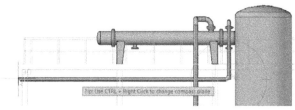

10. Change the view orientation to SW Isometric.

11. On the Status bar, click the down arrow next to **Object Snap** icon, and then select **Midpoint** from the menu.

12. Again, select the vertical portion of the pipe and click the Move Part grip located at the middle.

13. Move the pointer and select the midpoint of the horizontal pipe. The length of the horizontal pipe is changed.

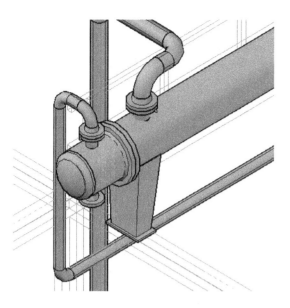

Creating Stub-in and Tee joints

A Stub-in joint creates a T-joint without using a fitting. This type of joint is useful if there are no fittings available for the selected pipe size.

1. Change the view orientation to Top.
2. On the ribbon, click **Home > Part Insertion > Route Pipe**.
3. Click **STub-in** in the command line.
4. Zoom to the pumps area and click on the midpoint of the pipe connecting the 6" nozzles.

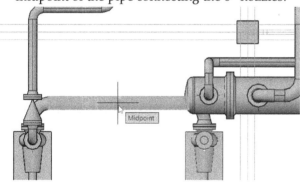

5. Move the pointer upward and click to create a stub-in joint.

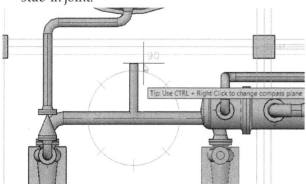

6. Press Esc to deactivate the active command.
7. Select the stub-in pipe and press Delete. The program deletes the stub-in joint.
8. Click on the pipe connecting the 6" nozzles. You notice a + mark at the middle.
9. Click on the + mark and move the pointer. A T-joint is created at the center.

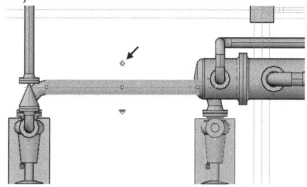

10. Move the pointer upward and click.

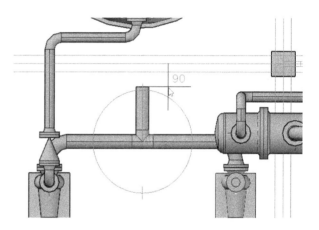

Creating Elbows and Pipe Bends

1. On the status bar, deactivate the **Ortho Mode** icon.
2. Rotate the pointer, and you notice the pipe rotates only at angle intervals (45, and 90).

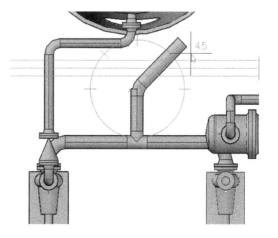

3. On the **Part Insertion** panel, click the **Toggle Cutback Elbows** icon. The program activates the cutback elbow mode. The cutback elbow mode is used to create elbows at non-standard angles.

4. Rotate the pointer, and you notice that the pipe is rotated freely.

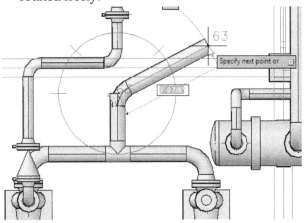

5. Turn on the Dynamic Input icon on the Status bar.

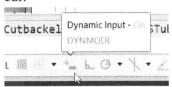

6. Press Tab key and type-in 68 in the angle box attached to the pipe.

7. Press Enter to create an elbow.

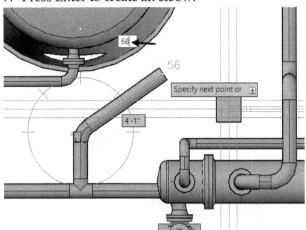

8. On the **Part Insertion** panel, click the **Toggle Pipe Bends** icon to activate the pipe bends mode.

In addition, the cutback elbows mode is deactivated.

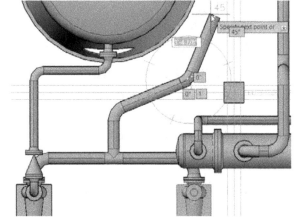

9. Rotate the pipe up to 45-degree angle and click to create a bend.

10. Press Esc to deactivate the active command.

11. Select the 45-degree bend; the two pipes connected to it are also selected.

12. Right click and select **Convert to Pipes and Bends** from the shortcut menu; the pulled pipe is converted into pipes and bends.

Creating Sloped Pipes

AutoCAD Plant 3D allows you to create sloped pipes.

1. On the **Slope** panel, type-in **1″** and **10″** in the **Slope Rise** and **Slope Run** boxes, respectively.

2. Click the **Toggle Slope** icon.

3. Create piping, as shown.

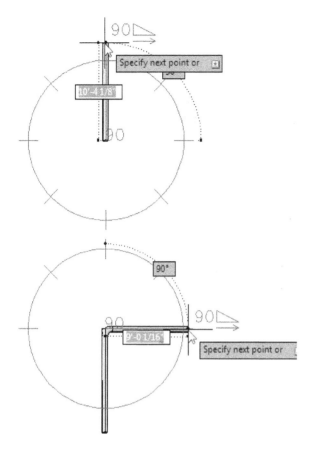

4. Change the view orientation to Front. You notice the sloped pipe.

You can also change the slope, but it may result in disconnected pipes.

5. Click the right mouse button on the sloped pipe and select **Pipe Slope Editing**.

On the **Edit Slope** dialog, you can redefine the slope of the pipe by calculating the **Start Elevation, End Elevation,** or **Slope angle**.

6. On the **Edit Slope** dialog, select **Calculation > End Elevation**.
7. Type-in 20 in the **Slope(degrees)** box and click **OK**. The **Slope Angle Exceeded** message box appears.
8. Click **Yes** to change the slope angle. This results in a broken connection.

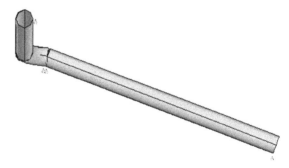

Creating offset piping
AutoCAD Plant 3D allows you to create pipes offset to a reference line.

1. Change the view orientation to Front.
2. Deactivate the **Toggle Slope** icon on the **Slope** panel.

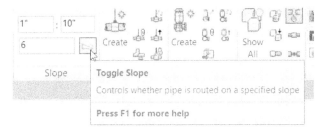

3. On the ribbon, click **Home > Part Insertion > Route Pipe**.

4. Click **routingOffset** in the command line.

5. Click **offsetDistance** in the command line.

6. Type 2'as the Horizontal distance and press Enter.

7. Type 2' as the Vertical distance and press Enter.

8. Select the grid points, as shown. You notice that the pipe is created at the specified offset distance from the select points.

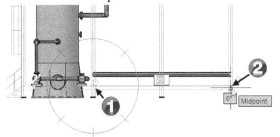

9. Move the pointer up and click.

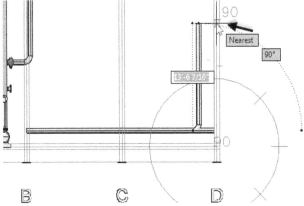

10. Change the view orientation to Top. You notice that the pipe is created at a horizontal offset as well.

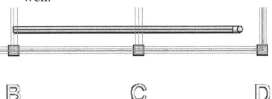

11. Press Esc to deactivate the active command.

12. To deactivate the offset routing, expand the **Elevation & Routing** panel and type-in 0 in the **Horizontal Offset** and **Vertical Offset** boxes.

13. Zoom to a pipes open end to notice the drop symbol, which indicates that the pipe is open. You can turn ON/OFF this symbol using the **Toggle Disconnect Markers** icon.

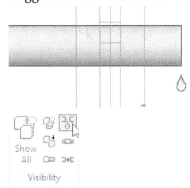

Adding Insulation and Welds to Pipes

1. Click the right mouse button on the pipe connected to the heat exchanger, and then select **Properties**.

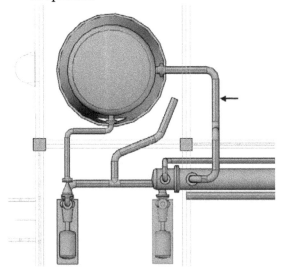

2. On the **Properties** palette, scroll down to the **Process Line** section, and set the **Insulation Thickness** and **Insulation Type**.

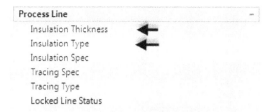

3. On the ribbon, click **Home > Visibility > Toggle Insulation Display** to display the insulation by increasing the thickness of the pipe.

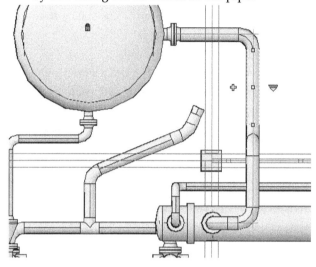

Welds are added by default when two pipe components are created continuously. However, you can add a weld when you want to break the pipe. To add welds, follow the steps given next.

4. Click the right mouse button on the pipe connecting the heat exchanger and vessel, and then select **Add Weld to Pipe**.

5. Move the pointer and click to define the location of the weld (or) type-in the distance value to locate the weld.

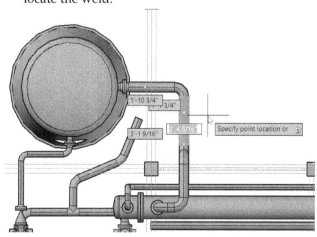

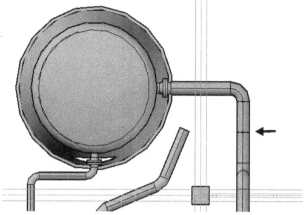

6. Click **eXit** in the command line.

Tutorial 10 (Adding Inline assets)

Before adding inline assets, create a pipe connection between the right pump and vessel.

1. Change the view orientation to **SW Isometric**.
2. On the **Part Insertion** panel, select **002** from the **Line Number Selector** drop-down.
3. Click on the right pump to highlight it.
4. Click on the + mark on the 4″ nozzle.

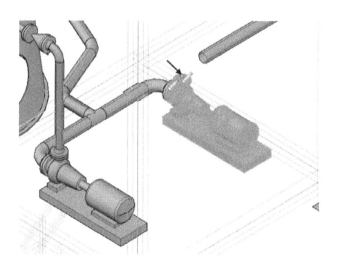

5. Move the pointer and select the midpoint of the elbow originating from the vessel.

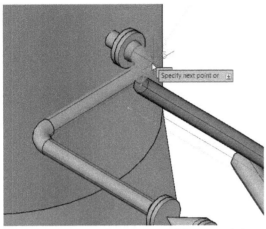

6. Click **Next** in the command line until the following solution is displayed.

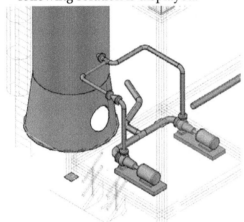

7. Click **Accept** to create the pipe connection.

After creating piping, you can add inline assets such as valves and fittings. There are three methods to add inline assets to the piping. Earlier, you have learned to add inline assets using the P&ID Line List palette. It is the best method to add pipe components to the 3D model as it links them to the corresponding P&ID symbols automatically. However, you can add inline assets using the Spec Viewer and Dynamic Tool Palette.

8. Make sure that the CS300 spec is loaded on the Dynamic Tool Palette.
9. On the Dynamic Tool Palette, scroll down to the **Valve** section and select **Globe Valve, FL, RF, 300, (CS300)**.

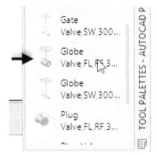

10. Move the pointer on the horizontal pipe connected to the right pump. You notice that the valve moves along the pipe.
11. Select the endpoint of the pipe. The valve is positioned at the selected point, and the compass appears. The valve rotates as you rotate the pointer.

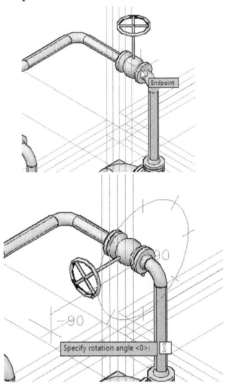

12. Press Enter to position the valve at the default angle.

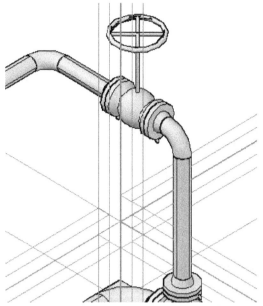

13. Press Esc.
14. Select the globe valve, click the right mouse button, and select **Properties**.
15. On the **Properties** palette, scroll down to the **Tag** section and click in the **Tag** box.
16. Click the icon next to the **Tag** box.

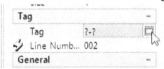

17. On the **Assign Tag** dialog, type-in HA and 102 in the **Code** box and **Number** boxes, respectively. Click **Assign**.

Editing Inline assets

1. Click the globe valve to highlight it. You notice many grips displayed on the valve.
2. Click on the circular grip and rotate the valve.
3. Type-in a new rotation value and press Enter.

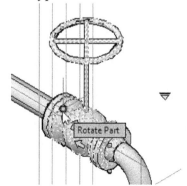

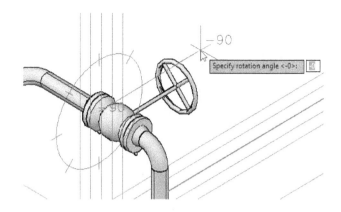

4. Again, select the globe valve and click on the vertical arrow grip. The grip flips the side of the valve.

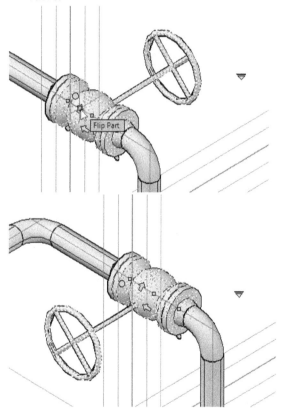

You can notice the three square grips displayed on the highlighted valve.

5. Click on the square grip of the valve, and then move the pointer. The valve moves along the pipe.

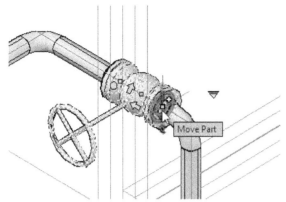

6. Click to define the new position of the valve or type-in the distance value to define the location.

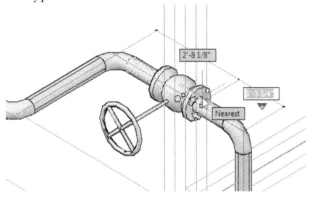

You can also place the valve on another pipe using the square grip.

7. Click on the check valve to highlight it.
8. Click on the horizontal arrow grip to flip the direction of the valve.

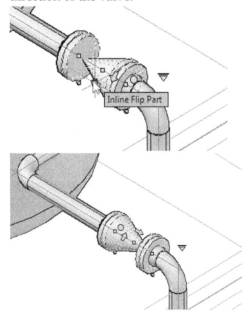

9. Click on the **Substitute Part** grip to open a menu. You can select the replacement part from this menu.

You can also change the valve operator.

10. Select the globe valve, click the right mouse button and select **Properties**.
11. On the **Properties** palette, scroll down to the **Valve Operator** section and click in the **Operator** box.
12. Click the icon next to the **Operator** box.

13. On the **Override Valve Operator** dialog, scroll right to see different operators.
14. Select the T-Crank operator and you notice the preview image along with dimensions.

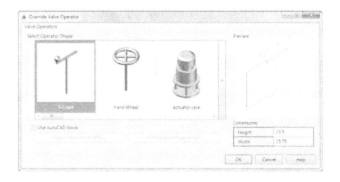

15. Type-in values in the **Dimensions** table and click **OK**. The operator of the globe valve is changed.

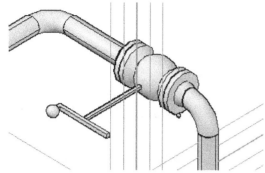

Adding Inline Assets at Pipe ends

1. Change the view orientation to NE Isometric.
2. Click on the vessel to highlight it.
3. Click the + mark on the 4″ nozzle and start routing.

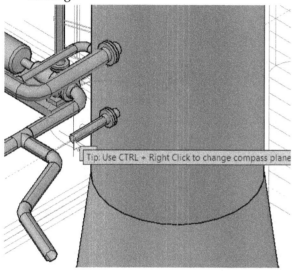

4. Click **pipeFitting** in the command line. The **Pipe Fittings** dialog appears. On this dialog, you can select the type of fitting.
5. On the dialog, click the **Flanges** button.
6. Select **Class Types > FLANGE BLIND**. A blind flange of 4″ size is available. If you want a flange of different and size, then click **Change** at the top of the dialog. The additional options appear to change the size, spec, and end type.

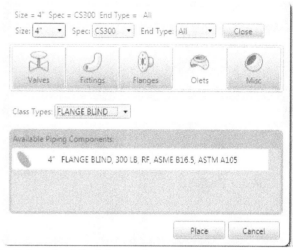

7. Select the blind flange from the **Available Piping Components** section and click **Place**. The blind flange is attached to the pipe end.
8. Move the pointer and click to create a pipe with a blind flange.

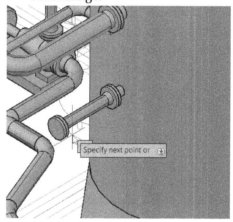

9. Press Enter to rotate the flange at the default angle.

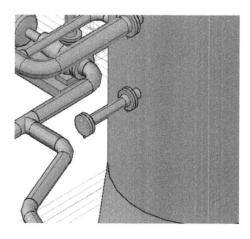

10. Select the pipe and blind flange, and then press **Delete**.

Adding Custom Parts

AutoCAD Plant 3D allows you to add custom parts to the 3D Model, which are not available in the selected spec file. You can also create your 3D blocks and add them to the Plant 3D model.

1. Change the view orientation to SW Isometric.
2. On the ribbon, click **Home > Part Insertion > Custom Parts**.

3. On the **CUSTOM PARTS BUILDER** palette, select **Part Type > Valve**.
4. Click **Plant 3D Shape** tab under the **Graphics** section.
5. Click the **Shape Browser** button to open the **Plant 3D Shape Browser** dialog.
6. Click **Advanced shape options** to view the additional options at the left side of the dialog.
7. In the additional options, click **PipeRunComponents > Valve**. Only the valves appear in the browser.
8. Click the **Inline Shapes** button. The inline valve shapes are displayed on the dialog.
9. Click the down arrow in the search bar and select **Beveled (BV)**. The dialog filters the shapes based on the selected end type.
10. Select **Inline Valve, Cone Style (FLG/BW/PE)** from the browser, and then click **OK**.

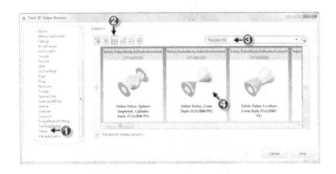

11. Under the **Part Properties** section, set **Tag** to **Do not prompt on Insert**.
12. Leave the default settings on the **CUSTOM PARTS BUILDER** palette and click **Insert in Model**.

13. Add the valve to the pipe connecting the heat exchanger.

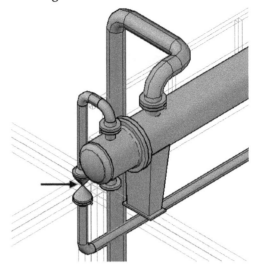

14. Press Esc twice.
15. Select the placeholder valve, click the right mouse button, and select **Properties**. The features of the valve appear in the **Properties** palette. You can change the dimensions of the valve, tag information, and other features.

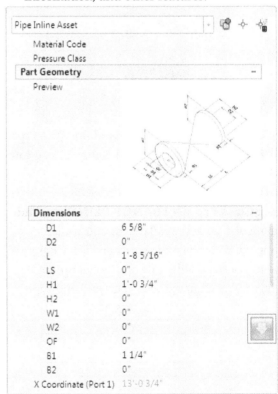

16. Select the custom valve and press **Delete**.

Tutorial 11 (Adding Pipe Supports)

After creating pipes, you can add pipe supports to them. The pipe supports are displayed in the isometric drawing.

1. On the ribbon, click **Home > Pipe Supports > Create**.

2. On the **Add Pipe Support** dialog, click the **Base Supports** icon.
3. Click the down arrow in the search bar and select **Clamped Supports**.
4. Select **Clamped Stanchion** and click **OK**.

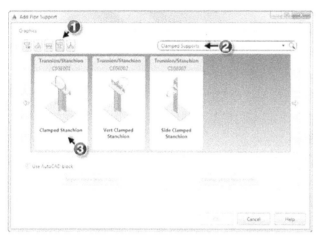

5. Move the pointer on the pipe, as shown. The pipe support aligns to the pipe.
6. Type-in a value (or) click at a point to define the location of the support.
7. Press Esc.

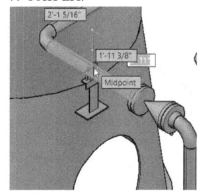

8. Change the view orientation to Left.
9. Click on the pipe support to highlight it.
10. Click on the down arrow grip located at the bottom of the pipe support.

11. Move the pointer down and click on the structural member located at the bottom. The program changes the elevation of the pipe support.

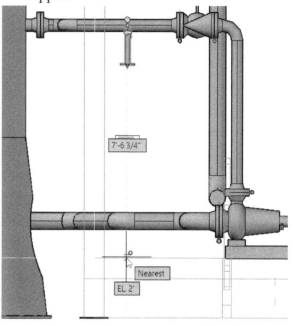

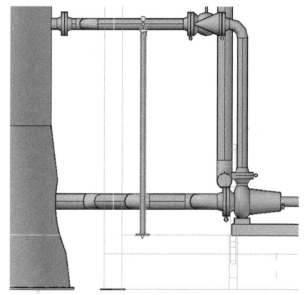

12. Save the file.

Tutorial 12 (Validating Project Drawings)

You need to validate a P&ID to check for errors. You can validate a single or multiple drawings in a project. Before validating a drawing, you need to set the type of errors to be check during validation. These errors include non-terminating lines, orphaned annotations, spec mismatches and more.

1. Switch to the **P&ID PIP** workspace.

2. Click the **Validate Config** button on the **Validate** panel of the **Home** ribbon; the **P&ID Validation Settings** dialog appears.

The dialog has four types of conditions to check for: P&ID objects, 3D Piping, Base AutoCAD objects, and 3D Model to P&ID checks.

You can select the type of errors to be checked by expanding the **P&ID objects** list. The P&ID is checked for errors such as size mismatches, spec mismatches, non-terminating lines and so on.

The **Size mismatches** option checks for schematic lines, which are connected to each other but are of different size.

The **Spec mismatches** option checks for schematic lines that are connected to each other but are of different spec.

The **Non-terminating lines** option checks for schematic lines that are not properly connected to the equipment or any component.

The **Unconnected components** option checks for equipments or components, which are not connected to any schematic lines. You need to make sure that there is atleast one connection To/From the component.

The **Flow direction conflicts** option checks for any two schematic lines which have opposite flow directions.

The **Orphaned annotations** option checks for tags that are placed far away from the components. You can specify the distance up to which the annotations can be placed. To do so, select the **Orphaned annotations** option and type-in a value in the **Orphaned Annotation Distance** box.

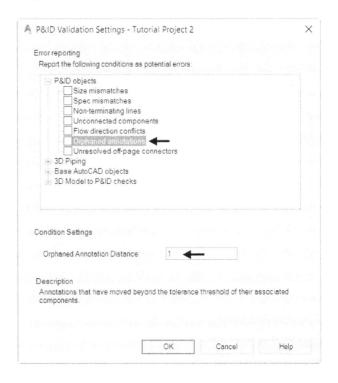

The **Unresolved off-page connectors** option checks for off-page connectors that are not connected to any other off-page connectors.

3. Check all the options under **P&ID objects**.

Expand **3D Piping** and you notice the **Disconnected port**, **Placeholder part** and **Property mismatch** options.

The **Disconnected port** option checks for pipes in 3D Piping model which are not properly connected to a component.

The **Placeholder part** option checks for parts, which are placed in a 3D Piping model, which are not available in the selected spec.

The **Property mismatch** option checks for pipe segments that are connected but have different properties.

4. Uncheck all the options under **3D Piping**.

Expand **Base AutoCAD objects** to check for AutoCAD objects. You can check for objects that are not created using P&ID tools. The base AutoCAD objects such as lines, polylines, circles, blocks, annotations, do not have any project data attached to them. The options under this node are very helpful to eliminate the unintelligent AutoCAD objects.

5. Uncheck all the options under **Base AutoCAD objects**.

Expand **3D Model to P&ID checks,** and notice the options to check the coordination between the P&ID objects and 3D Piping components. There are quite a few conditions to test the coordination between the P&ID and 3D Piping components. For example, if you have created a P&ID schematic line, but there is no piping component in the 3D model with the same properties (line tag), then an error appears. You can go through the other error types as they are self-explanatory.

6. Uncheck all the options under **3D Model to P&ID checks**.
7. Click the **OK** button on the **P&ID Validation Settings** dialog.
8. Click the **Run Validation** 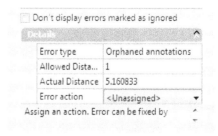 button on the **Validate** panel of the **Home** Ribbon; the validation starts and the **Validation Progress** dialog appears.

After completing the validation, the **Validation Summary** appears.

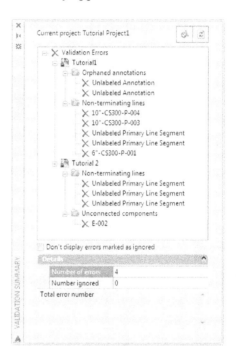

9. On the **Validation Summary** palette, under Tutorial 1, click the first **Unlabeled Annotation**. The orphaned annotation is highlighted in the drawing. The **Details** section on the **Validation Summary** palette shows the error type and the action to be taken. It also shows the actual and allowed distance between the component and tag.

Error type	Orphaned annotations
Allowed Dista...	1
Actual Distance	5.160833
Error action	<Unassigned>

Assign an action. Error can be fixed by

10. Under the **Details** section, click **Error action > Ignore**. The program ignores the selected error.

11. Check the **Do not display errors marked at ignored** option to hide the ignored errors.
12. Click the **Revalidate Selected Node** ⬚ icon on the **Validation Summary** palette.
13. Close the **Validation Summary** palette.

Validating the 3D model

1. On the **Project Manager**, click the right mouse button on **Tutorial Project** and select **Validation Settings**.
2. On the **Validation Settings** dialog, check all the options under **3D Piping** and **3D Model to P&ID checks** nodes. Uncheck all the options under **P&ID objects** and **Base AutoCAD objects** nodes, and then click **OK**.
3. Click the right mouse button on **Tutorial Project** and select **Validate Project**. The program performs validation and displays the validation summary.
4. Click **Tutorial 1 > Unmatched P&ID inline assets > HA-105** on the **Validation Summary** palette. The inline asset in the P&ID is highlighted because the pipe component corresponding to the P&ID asset is not placed in the 3D model. Under the **Details** section, you can find the description related to the error.

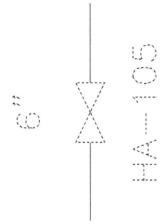

You can solve this error by placing a gate valve in the 3D model. You can use the P&ID Line list to place the gate valve.

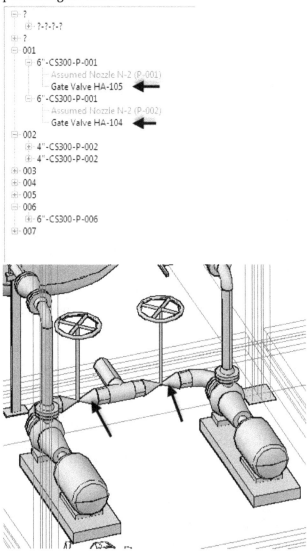

5. Likewise, solve the other errors or ignore them.

Tutorial 13 (Creating Isometric Drawings)

After creating a 3D model, you can create Isometric Drawings, which provide assistance in assembling the pipe components.

Specifying Iso Styles and other settings

In AutoCAD Plant 3D, the Isometric Drawings are created based on the project settings. You need to know about these settings so that you can modify the representation of the isometric drawings.

1. On the ribbon, click **Home > Project > Project Manager > Project Setup**.

2. On the **Project Setup** dialog, expand **Isometric DWG Settings** and select **Iso Style Setup**.

On the **Iso Style Setup** page, the **Iso Style** drop-down lists the Iso styles available. The **Check ANSI-B** Iso style is used to create isometric drawings. However, you can select other Iso styles. Click the + button next to the **Iso Style** drop-down, if you want to create a new Iso style.

The **Place field welds at maximum pipe lengths** option adds weld points on a long pipe based on the maximum length pipes that are available in the field. For example, if you have created a very long pipe in the model, but the available pipe length in the field is 25′ only. Then, you can check the **Place field welds at maximum pipe lengths** option and type-in 25′ in the **Maximum pipe length** box. The weld points are added in the isometric drawing at 25′ intervals on any pipe longer than 25′.

The **Add pipe makeup length to BOM for Field Fit Weld** option adds an extra pipe length to the bill of materials list to provide room for any adjustments in the field. Usually, the makeup length varies from 3″ to 1′.

In the **Table overflow** section, specify the action when a piping size is more than the sheet size. Instruct the system to overflow the drawing onto another sheet or split the isometric drawing.

The **File Naming** section has options to define the file name format. You can define the prefix of the file name format by using the **Prefix** box. You can add property to the prefix using the **Add Property** drop-down. For example, when you select the **Line Number** property from the **Add Property** drop-down, the line number property will be added to the isometric drawing name. You can use the **Delimiter** box to enter the delimiter. The **Suffix** drop-down has two options: **Numeric (01, 02, ...)** and **Alphabetic (A, B, ...)**. These options name the suffix based on the alphabetical or numeric systems. The naming format helps you while sorting drawings inside a folder.

If you want to create a spool drawing, then check the **Spool format** option. A spool drawing is created by dividing the piping into sections. It includes all the piping components and labels them. The spool drawing helps in assembling the parts correctly. You can notice that the **Table overflow** and **File naming** sections are grayed out as the piping is already broken into smaller parts in a spool drawing. The **Spool naming** drop-down has five options to define

the spooling format: **Numeric, Alphabetic, Line –
Numeric, Line – Alphabetic,** and **Use spool number
from the model.**

The **Sizing** drop-down in the **Spools** section has
three options. The **Automatic (Max. size)** option
checks the lengths of the pipes in the model and
generates a spool drawing based on them. The
Automatic (Max. weight) option creates the spool
drawing based on the pipe weight. The **Use spool
number from model** option uses the spool number
from the model to create the spool drawing.

Type-in values in the **Length, Width** and **Height**
boxes to define the area of the spool. The pipe layout
is broken into individual sections of a specified area.

The **Content paths** section is used to define the
locations for the production and quick isometric
drawings. These files are saved at default locations
under the project folder.

3. Click **Sloped and Offset Piping** under the tree.

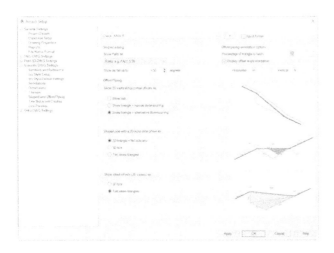

The **Sloped and Offset Piping** page has options to
define the display of sloped piping in the Isometric
drawings.

The **Show Falls as** drop-down has six options to
display the sloped piping: **Ratio, Angle, Percentage,
Gradient, Imperial incline, Metric incline,** and
Suppress falling Line Inclination. The last option
will not show any falling line indication.

The **Offset Piping** section has options to display
three types of offsets.

You can show 2D vertical/ horizontal offset using a
skew box.

The **Skew triangle + normal dimensioning** option
shows the 2D offset using the triangle and default
dimensions.

The **Skew triangle + alternative dimensioning**
option shows the 2D offset using the triangle and
alternative dimensions.

You can show the sloped piping with 2D horizontal
offset using a 2D triangle + fall indicator, 3D box, or
two skewed triangles.

The rolled offset (3D skews) can be shown using a
3D box or two skew triangles.

In the **Offset piping annotations options** section,
you can modify the annotation settings such as
percentage of a triangle to be hatched. The **Display
offset angle annotation** option can be used to turn
on/ off the offset angle annotation.

4. Click **Symbol and Reference** in the tree.

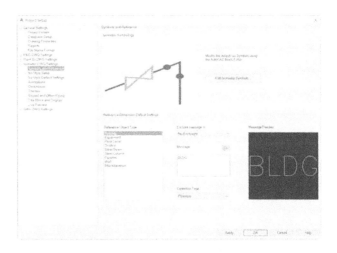

The options in the **Isometric Symbology** section
help you to change the display of the default
isometric fittings. To do so, click the **Edit Isometric
Symbols** button.

On the **Edit Block Definition** dialog, you can select the symbols to edit from the dialog. Click **Cancel** to exit this dialog.

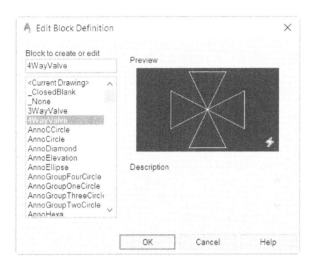

The options in the **Reference Dimension Default Settings** section help you to specify the display of the reference objects in the Isometric Drawing. For example, you can specify the way an equipment is displayed in the Isometric drawing. To do so, select **Equipment** from the **Reference Object Type** list.

Next, click the **Select Class Property** icon in the **Message** section. In the **Select Class Property** dialog, select a property from the **Property** list and click **OK**. The selected property will be displayed in the **Message** box. Also, the preview of the equipment message is updated. You can also select an enclosure for the message from the **Enclosure message in** drop-down.

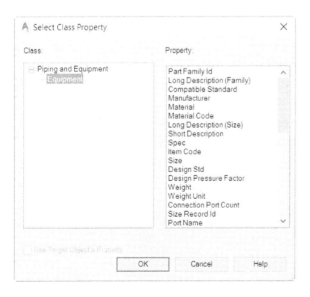

The **Centerline** drop-down is used to specify the way a centreline is displayed in the isometric drawing. You can select different line types such as Dashed/Existing, Centerline, Phantom, and so on.

5. Click **Title Block and Display** in the tree.

The **Elbow and bend display** section has options to modify the display of elbows and bends. The Insulation and pipe support display section has options to show or hide the pipe supports and insulation in the isometric drawing.

Annotation and Dimension settings

Annotations and dimensions settings of an Iso style are two of the most important settings.

1. Click **Annotations** under the tree.

On the **Annotations** page, the types of annotations that can be shown such as BOM, valve tags, cut pieces, welds, and spools are displayed.

The **BOM annotations** section has settings to define indexing, enclosure type, and type of leader line between the annotation and the part.

You can add prefixes such as F, G or B for part has flanges, gaskets or bolts, respectively.

If you check the **Spool**, **Weld**, and **Cut Pieces** options, then you can set the corresponding annotations.

In the **Connections and continuations** section, you can select various end connection annotations such as Iso sheet continuation, other connected pipelines, drains, vents, open pipe ends, or closed pipe ends. You can type-in connection prefix and text for each of the end connection type. In addition, you can attach coordinates and elevation values. The coordinate prefixes can be specified in the X, Y, Z boxes.

The **Valve tags** section has options to define annotation settings for control and non-control valves.

In the **Text** section, you can set the annotation text and enclosure height.

The **Use isometric planes** option, which is available in all the annotation sections, is used to set the orientation of the annotation in the isometric plane.

The **Expand Enclosures** option, which is available in all the annotation sections, is used to expand the callout enclosures to accommodate the text.

2. Click **Themes** under the tree.

There are three dimension types for an isometric drawing:

The **End to end (overall)** type dimensions option displays dimensions of complete pipe run.

The **String** type dimensions option adds dimensions to piping segments including fittings and inline accessories.

The **Locating** option adds a dimension to define the location of weld points or pipe supports from a specific point, such as the elbow.

As you check the dimension types one-by-one, they are displayed in the preview image. Each dimension type has a table to define the stopping point for different piping components.

You can also select a dimension theme from the Themes drop-down. A dimension theme is predefined setting to display particular dimensions only.

3. Click **Dimensions** under the tree.

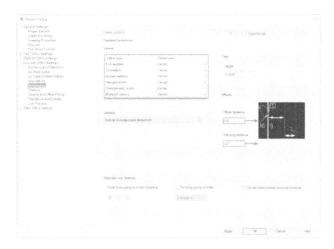

The **Valves** table defines the location of the dimensions for various valve types, such as Butt-welded, socket welded, thread, and so on.

The **Offsets** section has options to specify distances between the pipe lines and dimensions. Enter a value in the **Offset Distance** box to specify the distance between the pipe line and dimension. Likewise, enter a value in the **Stacking Distance** box to specify the distance between the stacked dimensions.

The **Gaskets** drop-down has three options: **Include in component dimension, Dimension gaskets individually** and **Do not dimension gaskets**.

The **Alternate Line Settings** section has some additional options. You can select the smallest bore piping to be included in the isometric drawing from the **Small bore piping up to and including** drop-down. Specify the status of the already existing piping using the **Existing piping includes** drop-down. Check the **Do not overconstrain the string dimensions** option to remove the last string dimension when you have an end to end dimension.

4. Click **OK** to close the **Project Setup** dialog.

Creating New Iso Styles

Earlier you have learned about various options of an already existing Iso Style. Now, you will learn to create a new Iso Style.

1. On the ribbon, click **Home > Project > Project drop-down > Project Setup**.
2. On the Project Setup dialog, expand the tree located at the left side and select **Isometric DWG Settings > Iso Style Setup**.
3. On the **Iso Style Setup** page, click the plus button located next to the **Iso Style** drop-down.
4. On the **Create Iso Style** dialog, enter **Custom** in the **Iso Style** name box.
5. Select **Create new Style**, and then click **Create.**

    The **Create Isometric Style** dialog appears. On this dialog, the **Table Layout and Paper Size** page appears. You can get more information about this page at the bottom of the dialog. On this page, notice the arrows available at the bottom. Use these arrows to explore different table layouts and sizes.

6. Click the right arrow located at the bottom to select the ANSI-B 4" layout.

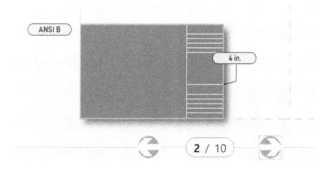

7. Click the right arrow located at the top.

    The **Leader lines & Enclosures** page appears. On this page, you select the annotation leader and enclosure settings. Click the arrows located at the bottom to explore the different leader line and enclosure settings.

8. Use the right arrow located at the bottom to go to the 10/10 leader line and enclosure settings.

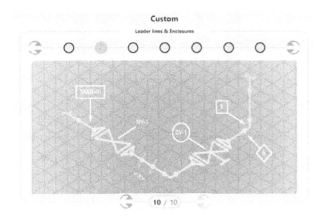

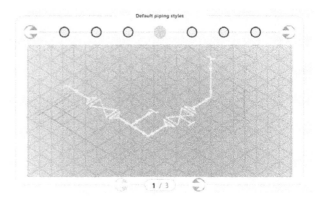

9. Click the right arrow located at the top to move to the next page.

    On the **Ribbon planes** page, you can specify the distance between the pipe lines and dimensions.

10. Explore the ribbon plane settings using the arrows located at the bottom.
11. Select the **1/3** setting.

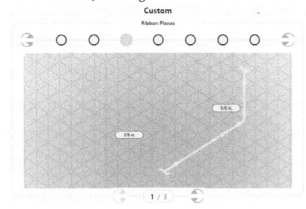

12. Click the right arrow located at the top to move the **Default piping styles** page.

    On the **Default piping styles** page, you can select the predefined dimension styles by clicking the arrows located at the bottom.

13. Select 1/3 setting.

14. Click the right arrow located at the top to move to the **Fitting-to-fitting piping styles** page.

    On the **Fitting-to-fitting piping styles** page, you can specify the dimension styles for fitting-to-fitting pipe runs.

15. Select the 2/3 setting.

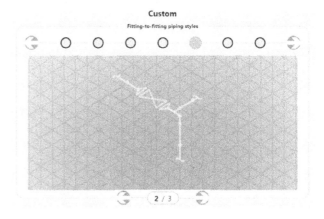

16. Click the right arrow located at the top to move to the **Small bore piping styles** page.
17. Select the 2/2 setting and move on to the next page.
18. On the **Text height & Symbol Scale** page, select the 1/4 setting.
19. Click **Create Style**.
20. Click **OK** to close the **Project Setup** dialog.

Generating a Quick Isometric Drawing

After configuring the Iso style and other project settings, you need to check whether the Isometric Drawing has all the information or not. The Quick Iso helps you to do this.

1. Activate the **3D Piping** workspace.

2. Change the **View Style** to **2D Wireframe**.

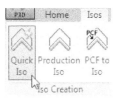

3. On the ribbon, click **Isos > Iso Annotations > Start Point** .

4. On the Status bar, click the down arrow next to the **Object Snap** icon and select **Endpoint** from the flyout.

5. Zoom to the left pump.

6. Place the pointer of the vertical pipe connected to the pump.

7. Select the end point of the centreline of the pipe.

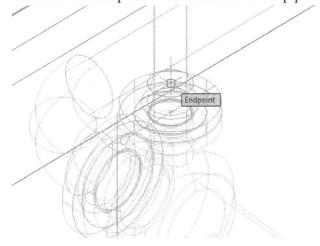

The start point is defined, as shown.

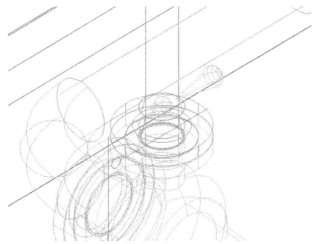

8. Change the **View Style** to **Realistic**.

9. On the ribbon, click **Isos > Iso Creation > Quick Iso**.

10. Select the pipe connections between the vessel and pumps. Also, select the pipe support and press **Enter**.

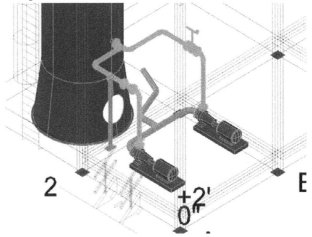

On the **Create Quick Iso** dialog, you can use the **Reselect** button to select the piping components again.

11. Select **Iso Style > Check_ANSI-B** from the dialog.

12. Click **Create** to generate the Quick Iso. The quick Iso is generated in the background. After few seconds, the **Isometric Creation Complete** balloon appears at the bottom right corner.

13. Click the link on the balloon to view the isometric creation details. The **Isometric Creation Results** dialog appears showing the warnings and the isometric drawing links.

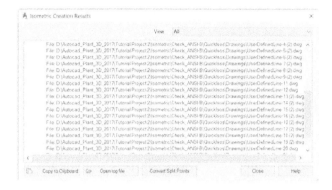

14. Click on anyone of the file links to open it. The isometric drawing appears (It may not be the same as that given below).

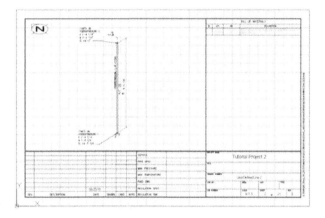

15. Review the Quick Iso and close it.

Creating Reference Dimensions

You can create reference dimensions to show the locations of the components such as structural members that cannot be documented in the Iso drawings.

1. Open the 3D piping model.
2. On the ribbon, click **Isos tab > Iso Annotations** panel **> Reference Dimensions**.

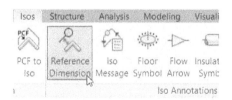

3. Set the view orientation to Top.
4. Select the horizontal pipe connected to left pump.

5. Move the pointer horizontally and select a point on the steel beam adjacent to the pump; a dimension appears between the selected points.

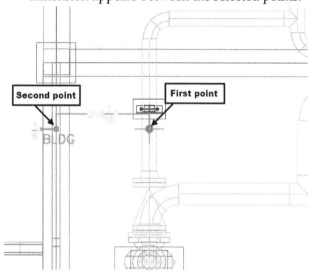

6. Select the dimension, right click, and select **Properties**.
7. On the **Properties** palette, scroll down to the **Reference Object** section.
8. In the **Reference Object** section, select **Steel Beam** from the **Object Type** drop-down.
9. Click in the **Message** field and press Backspace on the keyboard.
10. Type STR in the Message box.

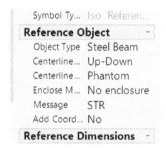

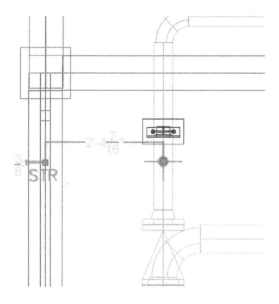

11. Save the 3D piping model file.

Generating Production Isometric Drawings

In AutoCAD Plant 3D, you can create Production Isometric drawings based on the 3D model.

1. On the ribbon, click **Isos > Iso Creation > Production Iso**.
2. On the **Create Production Iso** dialog, check 002 in the **Line numbers** section.
3. Set the **Iso Style** to **Final_ ANSI-B**.

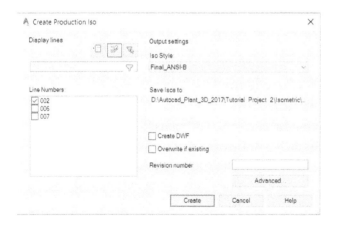

4. Leave the other default settings and click the **Advanced** button.

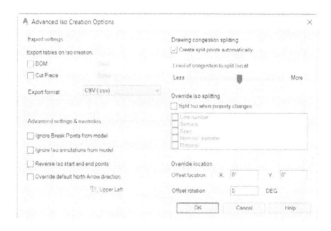

On the **Advanced Iso Creation Options** dialog, the **Export Settings** section has options to export the tables on the isometric drawing.

16. Check the **BOM** option and set the **Export format** to CSV(.csv).

The options in the **Override Iso splitting** section allow you to split a large Isometric drawing into small Isos. You can instruct the program to break the Iso if a property such as Line number or service changes.

17. Check the **Split Iso when property changes** option, and then check the **Line number** property.
18. Review the other settings on the dialog and click **OK**.
19. Click **Create** on the **Create Production Iso** dialog. The **Production Iso** generation runs in the background. A balloon appears after generating the Production Iso.
20. On the balloon, click the link to see the results.
21. Click on the first hyperlink on the **Isometric Creation Results** dialog. The isometric drawing includes details such as BOM, Cut Piece list, annotations and dimensions of the pipe components.

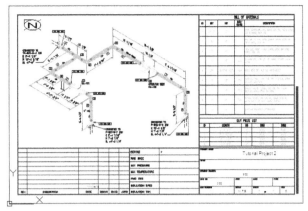

22. Click on the third hyperlink on the Isometric Creation Results dialog; the Isometric drawing appears along with the reference dimension.

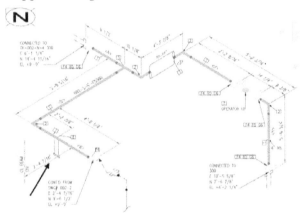

23. Close the isometric drawing.
24. On the ribbon, click **Isos > Iso Creation > Production Iso**.
25. On the **Create Production Iso** dialog, check 002 in the **Line numbers** section.
26. Set the **Iso Style** to **Spool_ ANSI-B**.
27. Click **Create**.
28. On the balloon, click the link displayed to see the results. You notice that there are four hyperlinks, which means that a separate drawing is created for each pipe.
29. Click on the first hyperlink on the **Isometric Creation Results** dialog.

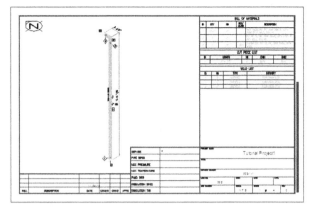

30. Click the **Isometric DWG** tab on the Project Manager and you notice that the drawings are arranged in a folder. You can access the isometric drawings from these folders.

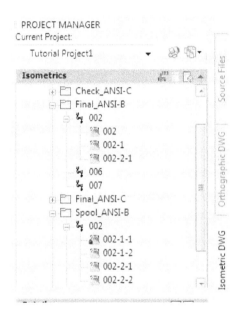

Adding Isometric Messages and Annotations

You can add some additional information to the Isometric drawings using symbols and messages. They are available on the **Iso Annotations** panel. They are inserted in the 3D model and visible in the Isometric drawings.

1. Set the **View Style** to **2D Wireframe**.

2. On the ribbon, click **Isos > Iso Annotations > Iso Message**.
3. On the **Create Iso Message** dialog, select **Box (Diamond end)** from the **Enclose message in** drop-down.
4. Type-in a message in the **Message** box and click **OK**.
5. Click on the pipe connected to the right pump, as shown. A sphere appears at the selected point.

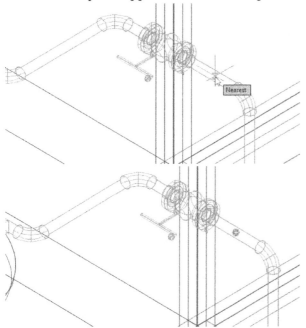

6. On the ribbon, click **Isos > Iso Annotations > Flow Arrow**.
7. Click on the pipe to define the insertion point, as shown.

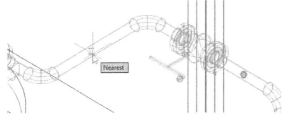

8. Click **Accept** in the command line. You can also click **Reverse** if you want to change the flow direction.
9. On the ribbon, click **Isos > Iso Annotations > Insulation Symbol**.
10. Click on the pipe, as shown.

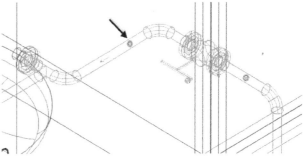

Likewise, you can add other symbols to the Isometric drawing.

11. Create a Quick Iso and view the results.

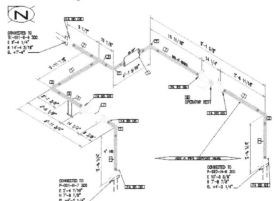

Export the Piping data to PCF format

You can export the piping data to a PCF (pipe component files), which helps you to use the information in other applications.

1. On the ribbon, click **Isos > Export > PCF Export**.
2. On the **Export PCF** dialog, check the 002 under the **Line Numbers** list. You can also define the file location using the **Save PCF files** to option.

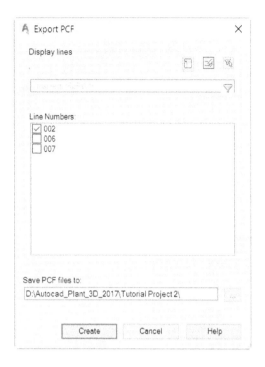

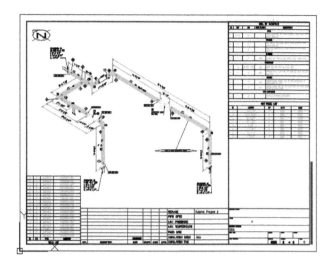

The Isometric drawing created from the PCF is not linked to the project.

12. Close the Isometric drawing.

Importing the PCF file into a 3D Model

In AutoCAD Plant 3D 2017, you can import PCF file and convert it into a 3D piping model.

1. Create a new Plant 3D drawing using the New button located on the Project Manager.
2. On the ribbon, click **Home** tab > **Part Insertion** panel > **PCF to Pipe**.
3. Browse to the location of the 002.pcf file.
4. Select the file and click **Open**.
5. Click the **Create Piping** button on the **PCF to Pipe** dialog; the PCF file is converted into 3D pipe.
6. Click **Close** on the dialog.

3. Click **Create** to complete the PCF creation.

Now, you can use the PCF file to create an Isometric Drawing.

4. On the ribbon, click **Isos > Iso Creation > PCF to Iso**.
5. On the **Create Iso from PCF** dialog, click the **Add** button.
6. Go to the location of the 002.pcf file.
7. Select the file and click **Open**.
8. On the dialog, select **Iso Type > Final_ ANSI-C**.
9. Click **Create** to create an Isometric Drawing from the PCF.
10. On the balloon, click on the link displayed to see the results
11. Click on the first hyperlink on the **Isometric Creation Results** dialog.

Locking Pipes after creating their Isometric Drawings

AutoCAD Plant 3D provides an option to lock the pipe number after generating its final Isometric

Drawing, which prevents anyone from changing the piping.

1. On the Project Manager, click the **Isometric DWG** tab.
2. Expand the **Final_ANSI-B** folder.
3. Click the right mouse button on 002 line number and select **Lock Line and issue**. The program locks the line number. If you want to unlock it, then click the right mouse button on it and choose **Unlock Line**.

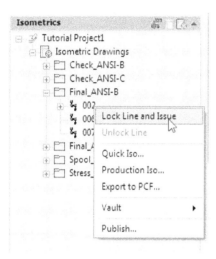

Tutorial 14: Creating Orthographic Drawings

AutoCAD Plant 3D allows you to create plan and elevation views using a 3D model. The changes in the 3D model are reflected in the views, automatically.

1. On the ribbon, click **Home > Ortho Views > Create Ortho View**.

The **Create Orthographic Drawing** dialog displays the already existing orthographic drawings.

2. Click **Create new** on **Create Orthographic Drawing** dialog.
3. On the **New DWG** dialog, type-in **Plan** in the File name box.

4. Click **OK**.

The **Ortho Editor** tab appears on the ribbon.

5. On the **Ortho Editor** tab, click **Ortho Cube > Top** to create the top view of the 3D model.
6. On the **Ortho Editor** tab, click **Select > 3D Model Selection**. The **Select Reference Models** dialog appears. This dialog is used to select the 3D models to include in the orthographic views.
7. Under the Project models section, make sure that **Master Model** is selected. Click **OK**.

8. On the **Output Appearance** panel, select **Hidden Line Piping** from the drop-down.
9. Make sure that the **Matchlines** and **Cut Pipe Symbol** icons are highlighted. These options turn ON the matchlines and cut pipe symbols.
10. Click the **Paper Check** icon to check the view with the paper size.

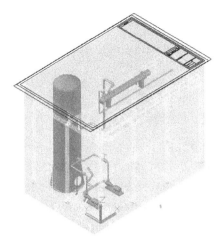

11. Set the **Scale** to ¼"=1'-0".
12. On the **Ortho Editor** tab, click **Library > Save Ortho Cube**.
13. On the **Save View** dialog, type-in **First Plan View** in the **View Name** box and click **OK**. The ortho cube settings are saved for future use.
14. On the **Ortho Editor** tab, click **Library > Load Ortho Cube**. On the **Load View** dialog, the **View List** displays the saved ortho cubes. You can select an ortho cube configuration to load it.
15. Close the **Load View** dialog.
16. Click **OK** on the ribbon and position the view on the paper space. The view is placed and a viewport is created.

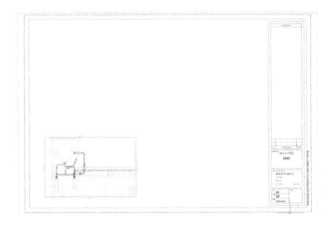

17. Double-click inside the viewport to activate it.
18. Select anyone of the objects in the viewport and notice that it is a block. These blocks are arranged in separate layers.

Creating Adjacent Views

1. On the ribbon, click **Ortho View > Ortho Views > Adjacent View**.

2. Select the viewport.
3. On the **Create an Adjacent View** dialog, select the **Front** view, and click **OK**. In the command line, notice the options to scale, rotate or use the settings of an existing view.
4. Place the pointer on the top-left corner point of the viewport and move it up. A trace line appears.
5. Click to place the front view.

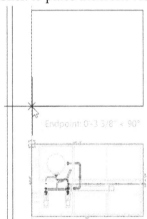

6. Activate the **Adjacent View** command and select the plan view.
7. On the **Create an Adjacent View** dialog, click **SW Isometric**, and then click **OK**.
8. Click on the paper space to position the Isometric View.

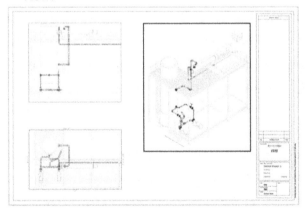

Editing Ortho Views

In the real world, there is always a need to modify the drawings. AutoCAD Plant 3D provides the essential tools to modify an update a drawing.

1. On the ribbon, click **Ortho View > Ortho Views > Edit View**.
2. Click on the plan view.
3. Click on the Ortho View cube in the **Orthographic View Selection** window. You notice various grips on the ortho cube. You can use these grips to modify the ortho cube.
4. Change the view orientation to Top.
5. On the ribbon, click **Ortho Editor > Ortho Cube > Add Jog**.

6. Click on the top horizontal edge of the Ortho View cube. A jog is added to it.

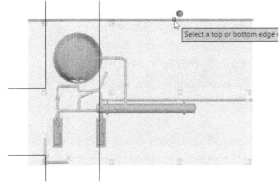

7. Click on the arrow that appears on the vertical edge of the jog.

8. Move it toward left and click to increase the jog width.

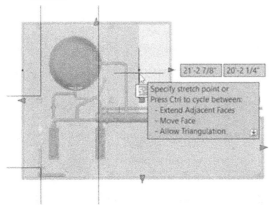

9. Likewise, modify the horizontal edge.

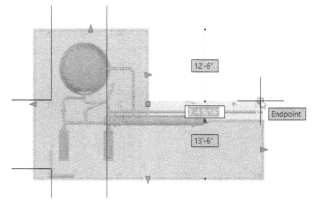

10. Click **OK** on the ribbon. The view is updated in the paper space.

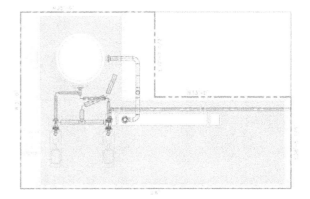

Updating and Deleting Ortho Views

Earlier you have learned to edit the ortho views. In addition to that, AutoCAD Plant 3D allows you to update the changes made in the 3D model.

1. Switch to the 3D Model file.
2. Click on the horizontal pipe connected to the heat exchanger.
3. Click the Move Part grip that appears at the middle of the pipe.

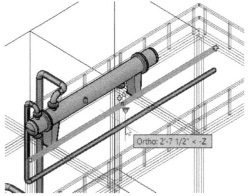

4. Move the pointer down and click to change the length of the vertical pipe connected to it.

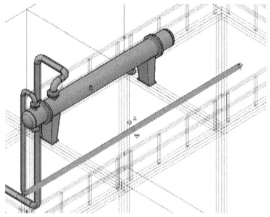

5. Save the 3D model and switch back to the ortho views file.
6. On the ribbon, click **Ortho View > Ortho Views > Update View**.
7. Click on the front view to update it.

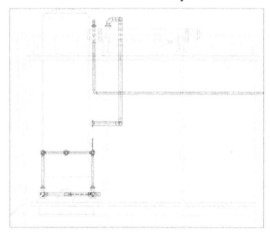

8. On the ribbon, click **Ortho View > Ortho Views > Delete View**.
9. Select the Isometric view to delete it.

Adding Bill of Materials

AutoCAD Plant 3D provides you with a couple of tools to define the BOM format, add and update BOM. These commands are located on the **Table Placement & Setup** panel.

1. On the ribbon, click **Ortho View > Table Placement & Setup > Table Setup**.
2. On the **Table Setup** dialog, click **Table type > Bill of Materials**. You can also select **Bill of**

Materials and cut list or Bill of Materials-itemized.

The **Bill of Materials** table type assigns a single ID to all the components having same properties and creates a BOM.

The **Bill of Materials and cut list** table type creates a BOM along with a cut list.

The **Bill of Materials-itemized** table type assigns a separate ID for each component and creates a BOM.

3. Click **BOM layout template > Grouped with category titles**.

The **Simple BOM** option creates a BOM without categorizing the components.

The **Grouped with category titles** option categorizes the BOM based on the component types (Pipes, fittings and valves).

The **Grouped with independent columns** option divides the BOM into separate categories. In addition, you have control over the columns displayed for each category. By default, the BOM displays only four columns (ID, QTY, ND, and DESCRIPTION). For example, if you want to display the MATERIAL column only for Fittings, then check the **MATERIAL** option for **Fittings**.

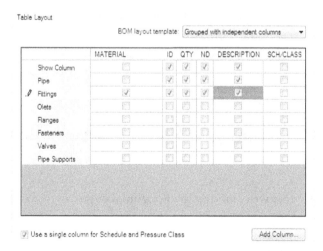

If you want to add a new column other than the existing ones, then click the **Add Column** button on the dialog. On the **Select Class Property** dialog, select the class and its related property.

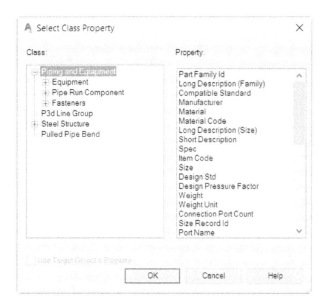

4. Click the **Settings** tab on the **Table Setup** dialog.

On the **Settings** tab, you can sort the BOM components in **Ascending Size** or **Ascending Description**. You can turn ON/OFF the display of cutback elbows and fixed length pipes. In addition, you can control the way a part **Description** is displayed.

5. Leave the default settings and click **OK**.

6. On the ribbon, click **Ortho View > Table Placement & Setup > Bill of Materials**.
7. Select the plan view.
8. Define the first and second corners of the BOM, as shown. The BOM is created.

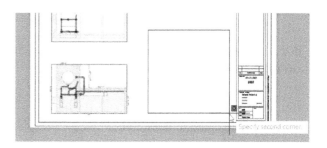

ID	QTY	NO	SCH/CLASS	DESCRIPTION
			PIPE	
1	82'-8 13/16"	1"		PIPE, SEAMLESS, PE, ASME B36.10, ASTM A106 Gr B SMLS, Sch 40
2	30'-9"	6"		PIPE, SEAMLESS, PE, ASME B36.10, ASTM A106 Gr B SMLS, Sch 40
			FITTINGS	
3	8	1"		ELL 90 LR, BW, ASME B16.9, ASTM A234 Gr WPB SMLS, Sch 40
4	1	1"		TEE, BW, ASME B16.9, ASTM A234 Gr WPB B16.9, Sch 40
5	8	6"		ELL 90 LR, BW, ASME B16.9, ASTM A234 Gr WPB SMLS, Sch 40
6	1	6"		TEE, BW, ASME B16.9, ASTM A234 Gr WPB SMLS, Sch 40
			FLANGES	
7	8	1"	300	FLANGE WN, 300 LB, RF, ASME B16.5, ASTM A106
8	4	6"	300	FLANGE WN, 300 LB, RF, ASME B16.5, ASTM A106
			FASTENERS	
9	8	1"	300	BOLT SET, RF, 300 LB, STUD BOLT
10	8	1"	300	GASKET, SWG, 1/8" THK, RF, 300 LB, ASME B16.20, CS/PTFE
11	4	6"	300	BOLT SET, RF, 300 LB, STUD BOLT
12	4	6"	300	GASKET, SWG, 1/8" THK, RF, 300 LB, ASME B16.20, CS/PTFE
			VALVES	
13	1	4"	300	Check Valve, Swing, 300 LB, RF, ASME B16.10, ASTM A216 Gr WPB
14	1	1"	300	Globe Valve, 300 LB, RF, ASME B16.10, ASTM A216 Gr WPB, Hand Wheel
			PIPE SUPPORTS	
15	1	6"		Custom Transition/Standfan

You can change the **Table Setup** anytime and use the **Update Bill of Materials** command to update the BOM.

Adding Annotations and Dimensions

In AutoCAD Plant 3D, annotations and dimensions are added at the final stages of the design. The annotation and dimensions commands are available on the **Annotation** panel.

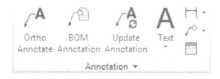

1. On the ribbon, click **Ortho View > Annotation > Ortho Annotate**.
2. Click in the top view and select the heat exchanger.
3. Press Enter to add the Equipment Tag.
4. Place the annotation below the heat exchanger.

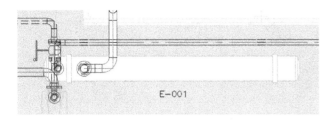

E—001

5. On the ribbon, click **Ortho View > Annotation > BOM Annotation**.

6. In the Bill of Materials, select a data element in the first row under the **Pipe** category. The balloon is attached to the pointer.

7. Position the balloon near the pipe to which it is attached. Another balloon is attached to the pointer as there are many pipes with the same size.

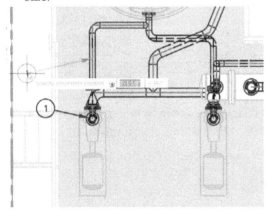

8. Press Esc to exit the balloon creation.

9. On the ribbon, click **Ortho View > Annotation > Linear**.

10. Zoom to the front view.

11. Use the Object Snap and select the endpoints of the horizontal pipe.

12. Move the pointer and position the dimension below the pipe.

Updating Dimensions

1. Click on the BOM table to highlight it.

2. Click the top left corner point of the BOM table and move it down.

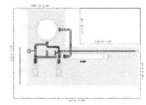 

3. On the ribbon, click **Ortho View > Ortho Views > Edit View**.

4. Select the front view.

5. On the **Ortho Editor** tab, set the **Scale** to 3/16" = 1'-0". Click **OK**.

The scale of the front view is changed. You notice that the dimension is not changed. The reason is that the dimensions are created on the paper space but not inside the viewport. You have to update the dimension manually.

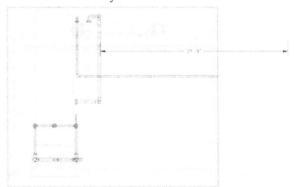

It is recommended that you add dimensions to the view at final stages as it requires a lot of rework to update them.

6. Select the dimension and press **Delete**.

Using the Locate in 3D Model and Pipe Gap commands

1. On the ribbon, click **Ortho View > Project Object Tools > Locate in 3D Model**.

2. Click on the left pump in the Top view. The Pump is highlighted in the model space.

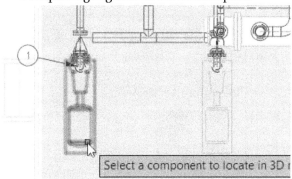

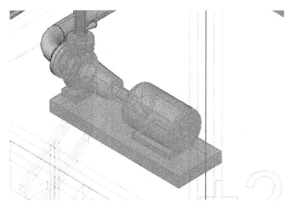

3. Click on the **Plan** tab to switch back to the Plan.dwg file.

4. On the ribbon, click **Ortho View > Project Object Tools > Pipe Gap**.

5. Zoom to the Front view and select the horizontal pipe. Two break symbols appear on the selected pipe.

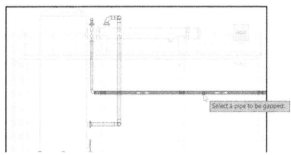

6. Increase the distance between the break symbols by dragging anyone of them. Press Esc.

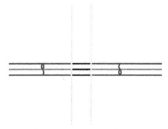

7. On the ribbon, click the **Update View** icon and select the Front view. The pipe gap is created.

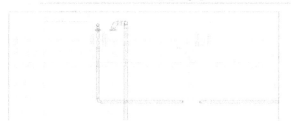

8. Save and close the drawing file.

TUTORIAL 15: (WORKING IN A PROJECT)

AutoCAD Plant 3D is a project-based application. Every object you create is stored in the project database. Therefore, it is very essential to know how to manage a project.

Using the Project Manager

The Project Manager helps you to create, open, add, and remove drawings from the project. The Project Manager appears at the left side of the screen. You can hide, close, or dock it to the application, but everything inside the Project is associated with it. There are quite a few options, which help you to organize files and perform additional operations related to project. Examine the options on the **Project Manager** as most of them are obvious.

If the **Project Manager** is not displayed, click **Home > Project > Project Manager**.

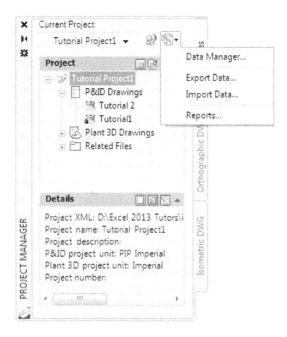

Changing the General Project Settings

The **Project Setup** dialog can be used to define or change the general project settings. It is recommended that you define the project settings while starting a project. However, here it is covered after basics.

1. On the ribbon, click **Home > Project > Project Manager > Project Setup**.
2. On the **Project Setup** dialog, expand **General Settings**. It has five sub-settings: **Project Details**, **Database Setup**, **Drawing Properties**, **Reports**, and **File name Format**.
3. Click **Project Details** under **General Settings**.

The **General properties** section on the **Project Details** page has **Project name**, **Project Description**,

and **Project Number** boxes. You can type–in the project description and number but cannot change the project name.

The **Work history prompts** section has **Opening project drawings**, **Closing project drawings** and **Never** options. If you select the **Closing project drawings** option, the program prompts you to enter the changes made to drawing before closing it.

4. Select **Closing project drawings** from the **Work history prompts** section.

The **General path and file locations** section has options to define the locations of the report files and other related files such as spreadsheets and text documents.

The **Custom properties** section has options to enter data related to different categories such as project and client. You can add a new category in addition to **Project data** and **Client Information** using the **Add** button.

There is a table showing the properties such as Address, City and State. You can add a new property to the table using the **Add row** button.

The **Tool palette group association** section helps you to set the P&ID and Piping tool palettes to be loaded when you open a file.

The **Interactive Zoom** section helps to set the zoom factor when you use the **Data Manager** to identify the components in the file.

5. Click the **Add** button in the **Custom properties** section.
6. Type **Contractor** in the **New category name** box and click **OK**.
7. Click the **Add Row** button to add a new field to the table.
8. On the **Add Row** dialog, type-in **Name** in the **Name** box and click **OK**. The **Name** property is added to the table.
9. Likewise, add the **Address** and **Telephone** properties to the table.

10. Click **Database Setup** under **General Settings** node.

The **Database Setup** page has two types of databases: **SQLite local database** and **SQL server database**. The database settings are defined while starting a project. If you want to change the database, then click the **Learn More** link on the dialog.

11. Click **Drawing Properties** in the **General Settings** node. On the **Drawing Properties** page, you can use the **Add** button to add custom properties to a drawing.
12. Click the **Add** button and type-in **Custom Properties** in the **New category name** box. Click **OK**.
13. Click the **Add Row** button.
14. On the **Add Row** dialog, type-in **Job Name** in the **Name** box and click **OK**.
15. Likewise, add the **Job Number** property.
16. Click **Reports** under **General Settings**. On the **Project reports** page, you can add, delete or modify a project report type.
17. Click **File name format** under **General Settings**.
18. Click the **Add** button on the **File name format** page.
19. Type-in **Discipline** in the **Name** box.
20. Set the **Type**, **Length** and **Delimiter** to **String, 2** and **-**, respectively.
21. Likewise, add two more fields, as shown.

22. Click **OK** on the **Project Setup** dialog.
23. Select the **P&ID Drawings** folder in the **Project Manager** and click the **New Drawing** icon. The **New DWG** dialog appears with three fields that you have created. You can check the **Override** option if you want to create a file without any naming format.

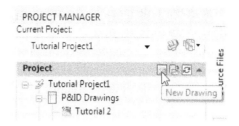

24. Type-in D, 6 and 001 in the **Discipline, Sheet Type,** and **Sheet Sequence**, respectively. Click **OK**.
25. The D-6-001.dwg file is added to the **P&ID Drawing** folder.
26. In the Project Manager, click the right mouse button on D-6-001 and select **Properties**. On the **Properties** dialog, notice the **Custom Properties** section. It has the **Job Name** and **Job Number** properties.

27. Click **OK** on the **Drawing Properties** dialog.

28. Double-click in the Title block of the drawing sheet to deactivate the viewport.
29. Type-in FIELD in the command line and press Enter.
30. On the **Field** dialog, click **Field category > Project**.
31. Select the **Project** from the **Field names** section.
32. Set **Format** to **Uppercase** and choose **ContractorName** from the **Property** list.

33. Click **OK** and place the property text on the **Title block**, as shown.

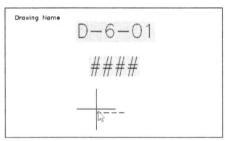

34. To enter a value for the property, click the right mouse button on **Tutorial Project** in the Project Manager, and select **Properties**.
35. On the **Project Setup** dialog, click **Project Details** in the **General Settings** node.
36. Under the **Custom properties** section, select **Contractor** from the **Custom categories** list and type-in **Matt** in the **Name** box.

37. Click **OK** and type-in **REGEN** in the command line. Press Enter to see the property value.

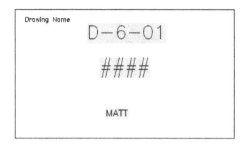

38. Add two pumps to the drawing, save and close it. The **Work History** dialog appears.
39. On the **Works History** dialog, set the **Status** to **In progress** and type **Added two pumps** in the **Notes** box. Click **OK**.

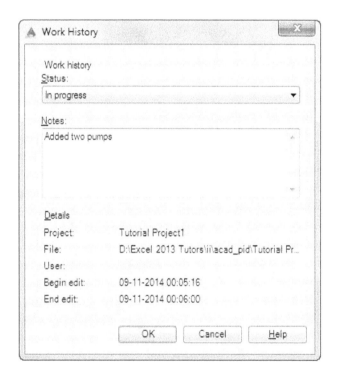

Using the Locate Drawing option

The **Locate Drawing** option can be used to locate lost files. To know how to use this option, you need to dislocate a drawing file.

1. Close the **AutoCAD Plant 3D** application window.
2. Go to the **Tutorial Project** folder. Under the PID DWG folder, create a new folder.

3. Manually relocate the drawings from the PID DWG to the new folder.
4. Start AutoCAD Plant 3D 2017.
5. Set the **Tutorial Project** as current.
6. Expand the **P&ID Drawings** folder. You will notice that the files are marked red.

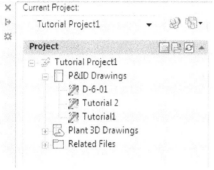

7. Click the right mouse button on the drawing and select **Locate Drawing**.

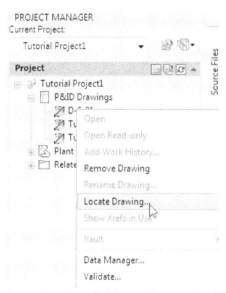

8. Go to the **New folder** and select the file.
9. Click **Open**. Now, you can open the drawing.

Using the Resave All Project Drawings option

The **Resave All Project Drawings** option can be used to save all the project drawings at a time. This option is very useful as it saves your time. However, it cannot save the file, which is opened by two or more users at a time. To save all the files that are currently

opened only on your workstation, click the right mouse button on the **Tutorial Project** and select **Resave all Project Drawings**.

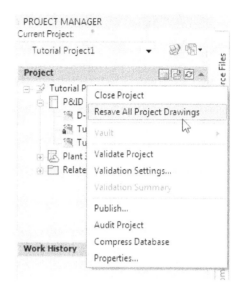

Using the Export to AutoCAD option

As the name says, the **Export to AutoCAD** option can be used to export the drawing files to AutoCAD format.

1. Open the **Tutorial 1** file from the **Project Manager**.
2. Click the right mouse button on Tutorial 1 and select **Export to AutoCAD**. The **Export to AutoCAD** dialog appears.

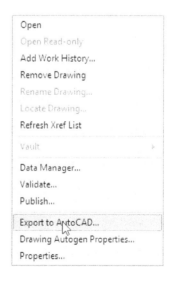

3. Go to the **Tutorial Project** folder.
4. Type **Tutorial1-exported** in the **File name** box.
5. Click **Save** to export the file.

6. On the **Quick Access Toolbar**, click the **Open** icon.
7. Open the exported drawing file.
8. Click the right mouse button on the vessel and select **Properties**. On the **Properties** palette, you can notice that the object is converted into a block reference. The P&ID properties of the object are not available, as it is no more linked to the project database.

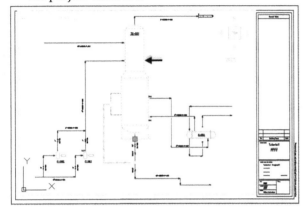

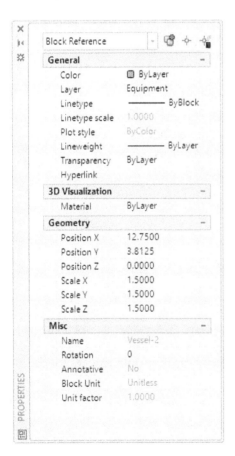

9. Likewise, you can export the Plant 3D drawings as well.

You can also export the project files into another format. To do this, click the **Application** icon located at the top left corner and select **Export > Other Formats**. On the **Export Data** dialog, select the format from the **Files of type** drop-down.

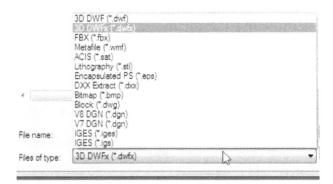

Tutorial 16 (Publishing and Printing)

You can produce a physical copy of a drawing, or publish it in electronic forms such as DWF, DWFx or PDF.

Publishing a Drawing to DWF format

1. On the **Project Manager**, click the right mouse button on the **P&ID Drawings** folder and select **Publish**.

2. On the **Publish** dialog, click the **Publish Options** button.

3. On the **Project Publish Options** dialog, under **P&ID DWF Options** section, click the icon next to the **P&ID Information** drop-down.

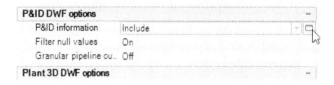

The program opens the **P&ID DWF Output Settings** dialog. The **Object Properties** tab helps you to control the symbol properties to be published. For example, select **Engineering Items > Equipment > Heat Exchangers > TEMA type BEM Exchanger**. The properties of the heat exchanger appear in the **TEMA type BEM Exchanger Properties** section. By default, all the properties are checked. You can uncheck the properties to be excluded from the output.

The **Sheet Properties** tab helps you to control the project details and drawing properties to be published.

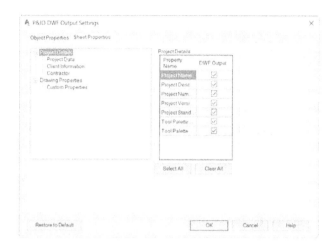

4. Click **OK** on the **P&ID DWF Output Settings** dialog.
5. Set the **P&ID Information** to **Include**. The program publishes the **P&ID information** along with the drawing.
6. Set the **Filter null values** to **On** to exclude the P&ID properties without any value.
7. Leave **Granular pipeline output** to **Off** to publish the pipe segments as a single output.
8. Leave the **Plant 3D DWF options** as default. These options are self-explanatory.
9. Under the **Default output location (plot to file)** section, click the icon next to the **Location** drop-down.
10. Go to the project folder location and click **Select**.
11. Under the **General DWF/PDF options** section, set the type to **Multi-sheet file**. The program creates a multi-sheet file.
12. Set **Naming** to **Prompt for name**. The program prompts you to provide the name while publishing the drawing.
13. Set **Layer** to **Include** to publish the drawing along with layer information.
14. Likewise, examine the other options on this dialog. Place the pointer on each option to get a brief explanation of it.

The options under the **3D DWF Options** section are available only while publishing drawings with 3D objects.

15. Click **OK** to close the dialog.
16. Select D-6-01 from the sheet list and click the **Remove Sheets** [ ] icon. Likewise, you can add sheets to the list using the **Add Sheets** [ ] icon.
17. Select **Tutorial 2-Model** from the sheet list and click **Move Sheet Down** [ ]. This action moves down the selected drawing.

On the **Publish** dialog, the **Sheet List** drop-down shows a sheet set. You can also create a sheet set using **Save Sheet List** icon next to the drop-down.

18. Click the **Save Sheet List** [ ] icon next to the **Sheet List** drop-down.
19. Save the sheet list as **PID Drawing.dsd**. The P&ID drawings listed on the **Publish** dialog are saved as a list.
20. Select **DWF** from the **Publish to** drop-down.
21. Select **Precision > For Civil Engineering**. You can also choose **Manufacturing** or **Architecture** (or) create custom precision. It depends on the precision that is required.
22. Uncheck the **Publish in background** option and check **Open in viewer when done** option.
23. Click **Publish** and save the file as **Tutorial Project.dwf**.

Publish a Drawing using Page setup

1. Open the **Tutorial 1** file.
2. Click the **Application Menu** icon at the top left corner and click **Print > Page Setup**.

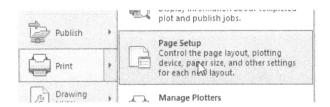

3. On the **Page Setup Manager** dialog, click the **New** button.
4. Type-in **Project Print Setup** in the **New page setup name** box and click **OK**.
5. Select a printer from the **Name** drop-down.

6. Set the **Paper Size** to **ANSI D (34.00 x 22.00 Inches)**.
7. Set the **Plot area** to **Layout**.
8. Make sure that the **Plot Style** is set to **PID.ctb**. The program prints the drawing using the P&ID color dependent lineweights.
9. Set the **Scale** to **1:1** and check the **Scale lineweights** option.
10. Leave the other default options and click **OK**.
11. Click **Set Current** and close the **Page Setup Manager** dialog.
12. Save the drawing.
13. Click the **Application Menu** icon and select **Publish**.
14. On the **Publish** dialog, select **Plotter named in page setup** option from the **Publish to** drop-down.
15. Select **Tutorial 1-Model** from the sheet list and click **Remove Sheets** [ ].
16. Select **Project Print Setup** from the **Page Setup** drop-down.

17. Click **Publish** to publish the document.
18. Likewise, you can print or publish Isometric, orthographic or Plant 3D drawings.

Index

www.ingramcontent.com/pod-product-compliance
Lightning Source LLC
Chambersburg PA
CBHW080423060326
40689CB00019B/4358